All About Niagara Falls: A Kid's Guide to North America's Most Famous Waterfall

Educational Books For Kids, Volume 9

Shah Rukh

Published by Shah Rukh, 2024.

While every precaution has been taken in the preparation of this book, the publisher assumes no responsibility for errors or omissions, or for damages resulting from the use of the information contained herein.

ALL ABOUT NIAGARA FALLS: A KID'S GUIDE TO NORTH AMERICA'S MOST FAMOUS WATERFALL

First edition. September 20, 2024.

Copyright © 2024 Shah Rukh.

ISBN: 979-8227852144

Written by Shah Rukh.

Table of Contents

Prologue

Welcome to the exciting world of Niagara Falls! Imagine standing next to a giant waterfall so powerful that the ground trembles beneath your feet and the air is filled with a cool mist. This is Niagara Falls, one of the most amazing natural wonders in North America, and it's been capturing the imaginations of people for centuries.

In this book, we'll take a journey through everything that makes Niagara Falls so special. From the moment the first drop of water began its journey over the cliffs thousands of years ago to the thrilling stories of the brave daredevils who've taken on the falls, there's so much to discover. You'll learn how the falls were formed, meet the animals that live in the surrounding areas, and find out how Niagara Falls helps power our world today.

Whether you're planning a visit or just curious to know more, this guide will make you feel like an expert on all things Niagara. Get ready for an adventure filled with fascinating facts, fun stories, and breathtaking moments as we explore the incredible Niagara Falls together!

Chapter 1: Discovering Niagara Falls

Niagara Falls is one of the most awe-inspiring natural wonders in the world, a place where the power of nature is on full display, captivating visitors with its breathtaking beauty and the thunderous roar of water crashing down over the falls. Located on the border between the United States and Canada, Niagara Falls is actually made up of three separate waterfalls: the Horseshoe Falls, the American Falls, and the smaller Bridal Veil Falls. Together, these waterfalls create an extraordinary spectacle that has drawn millions of visitors for centuries, with each fall having its unique features and charm.

Discovering Niagara Falls begins with an understanding of its immense scale and geological history. The falls were formed over 12,000 years ago, during the last Ice Age, when melting glaciers created the Great Lakes. Water from these lakes began flowing toward the Atlantic Ocean through the Niagara River, carving out the Niagara Gorge in the process. The relentless force of this water, combined with the soft rock beneath, caused the river to erode over time, eventually creating the falls we know today. This dynamic geological process continues even now, as the falls gradually move backward, retreating at an average rate of about one foot per year due to the constant erosion caused by the flowing water.

The most iconic and largest of the three waterfalls is Horseshoe Falls, named for its distinctive curved shape. This waterfall straddles the border between the United States and Canada, with the majority of its water flowing on the Canadian side. Horseshoe Falls is approximately 2,700 feet wide and 167 feet tall, making it the most powerful waterfall in North America in terms of water flow. An incredible 90% of the Niagara River's water rushes over Horseshoe Falls, creating a thunderous sound and a perpetual mist that rises high into the air, forming rainbows on sunny days. The sheer volume of water — approximately 681,750 gallons per second — that cascade over

Horseshoe Falls is a mesmerizing sight, and it has made this section of Niagara Falls the most popular and photographed by tourists.

While Horseshoe Falls is the largest, the American Falls, located entirely on the U.S. side of the border, offers a different but equally stunning view. The American Falls is about 940 feet wide and 100 feet tall, making it smaller than Horseshoe Falls but still an impressive sight. Unlike the smooth curve of Horseshoe Falls, the American Falls has a more rugged, straight-edged appearance, with large boulders at its base that have fallen from the cliffs above due to erosion. These boulders create a natural barrier, breaking up the water flow and giving the American Falls a distinct, choppy look. The water that flows over the American Falls comes from the upper Niagara River and is diverted by Goat Island, a small island that separates the American Falls from Horseshoe Falls. The sound of the water crashing onto the rocks below adds to the dramatic atmosphere, creating a sense of raw, untamed natural beauty.

Bridal Veil Falls, the smallest of the three waterfalls, is located to the right of the American Falls, separated by Luna Island. Although much smaller than its neighbors, Bridal Veil Falls is no less enchanting, with its delicate, veil-like cascade of water giving it its name. At only about 56 feet wide and 78 feet tall, Bridal Veil Falls may be the least powerful of the falls, but its charm lies in its serene, graceful flow. Visitors can get up close to Bridal Veil Falls by taking a walk across a pedestrian bridge that leads to Luna Island, where they can feel the cool mist and hear the soothing sound of the water.

Niagara Falls is not just a spectacle of nature; it is also a rich cultural and historical landmark. For thousands of years, Indigenous peoples of the region, such as the Seneca and Mohawk tribes, revered the falls for its spiritual significance and used it as a meeting place for trade and ceremonies. The name "Niagara" is believed to have originated from the Iroquoian word "Onguiaahra," which means "the strait" or "thunder of waters," reflecting the deep connection the Indigenous people had with the land and its natural features.

The falls gained international fame in the early 19th century when European settlers and explorers began to visit the area, marveling at its beauty. One of the most famous early visitors was French explorer Father Louis Hennepin, who is credited with being the first European to document Niagara Falls in the 1600s. His vivid descriptions of the falls, along with detailed illustrations, helped spread word of the majestic waterfall across Europe, drawing even more attention and inspiring adventurers and tourists to visit.

In the centuries that followed, Niagara Falls became a symbol of both natural beauty and human ingenuity. The falls have long been a popular destination for honeymooners, who are drawn to the romantic setting of the mist and the sound of rushing water. In fact, Niagara Falls has often been referred to as the "Honeymoon Capital of the World," with couples from all over traveling to the falls to experience its breathtaking views. The tradition dates back to the early 1800s, when the future First Lady of the United States, Theodosia Burr Alston, is said to have taken one of the earliest recorded honeymoons at Niagara Falls, sparking a trend that has continued to this day.

Beyond its romantic allure, Niagara Falls has also played a significant role in the development of modern engineering and technology. The powerful flow of the falls has long been harnessed for hydroelectric power, with the first hydroelectric power station built on the Niagara River in 1881. This early station, developed by inventor Thomas Edison and industrialist George Westinghouse, marked a major milestone in the use of electricity and paved the way for Niagara Falls to become a critical source of renewable energy. Today, the falls continue to generate hydroelectric power for both the United States and Canada, with massive power plants located on either side of the border. The harnessing of Niagara Falls for energy has helped fuel industrial growth in the region and remains an important part of the local economy.

While discovering Niagara Falls, visitors are also treated to a wide range of activities and attractions designed to enhance their experience of this natural wonder. One of the most popular ways to experience the falls up close is by taking a boat tour on the famous "Maid of the Mist." These boat tours have been operating since the mid-19th century and offer an exhilarating journey into the heart of the falls, where passengers are surrounded by the roar and mist of the cascading water. The boats travel past the American Falls and into the basin of Horseshoe Falls, where visitors can feel the full force of the water's power. It's an unforgettable experience that allows visitors to get as close to the falls as possible, creating lasting memories.

For those who prefer to stay on land, there are numerous observation points and parks that offer stunning views of Niagara Falls from different angles. In Canada, Queen Victoria Park is a popular spot for visitors to take in panoramic views of the falls, while on the U.S. side, the Niagara Falls State Park offers miles of walking trails that lead to scenic overlooks and picnic areas. For a bird's-eye view, visitors can also ride the Niagara SkyWheel, a giant Ferris wheel located in Clifton Hill, or take a helicopter tour for a breathtaking aerial perspective.

At night, Niagara Falls transforms into an even more magical sight, as colorful lights illuminate the water, creating a mesmerizing display. The nightly illumination of the falls has become a major attraction, with special light shows and fireworks displays held during the summer months and on holidays. The combination of the natural beauty of the falls and the vibrant light displays creates a surreal and unforgettable experience for visitors.

As visitors discover Niagara Falls, they are not only witnessing one of the most beautiful places on Earth but also experiencing the rich history, culture, and scientific importance that have shaped this extraordinary destination. Whether marveling at the sheer power of the water, exploring the surrounding natural beauty, or learning about its fascinating history, Niagara Falls offers an unforgettable journey into the heart of nature's majesty. It is a place where the forces of nature and human achievement converge, leaving a lasting impression on all who visit.

Chapter 2: The Formation of Niagara Falls

The formation of Niagara Falls is a fascinating journey into the depths of geological time, revealing the incredible forces of nature that shaped one of the most iconic landmarks on Earth. To understand the formation of Niagara Falls, one must first go back more than 12,000 years to the end of the last Ice Age, when much of North America was covered in massive glaciers. These glaciers played a pivotal role in shaping the landscape of the region, including the formation of the Great Lakes and, ultimately, the majestic Niagara Falls.

During the Ice Age, the Earth was locked in a deep freeze, with enormous ice sheets, some of them several miles thick, covering vast portions of the Northern Hemisphere. As temperatures gradually began to rise, the glaciers started to melt, releasing massive amounts of water into the surrounding areas. This meltwater from the glaciers carved out large basins in the landscape, which eventually became the Great Lakes: Lake Superior, Lake Michigan, Lake Huron, Lake Erie, and Lake Ontario. The water from these lakes needed an outlet to flow toward the Atlantic Ocean, and it found this path through the Niagara River, which connects Lake Erie to Lake Ontario.

The Niagara River is an integral part of the Niagara Falls story because it is this river that carries the water over the edge of the falls. The force of the water flowing through the river has been a constant for thousands of years, shaping the land and gradually forming the waterfalls we see today. However, the process of forming the falls was not instantaneous; it was a slow and steady transformation that took place over millennia, influenced by geological factors such as erosion, rock composition, and the unique geography of the region.

As the glacier meltwater continued to flow through the Niagara River, it encountered different types of rock layers. The uppermost layer of rock in the Niagara Gorge, where the falls are located, is composed of hard dolomite, also known as Lockport Dolomite. Beneath this dolomite layer is a softer type of rock known as shale, which erodes more easily when exposed to the force of water. Over time, the fast-flowing water of the Niagara River began to erode the softer shale layers beneath the dolomite, causing the harder dolomite rock above to crack and eventually collapse. This process created the steep cliffs and escarpments that are characteristic of the Niagara Gorge and the falls themselves.

This erosion process is a key factor in the formation of Niagara Falls and continues to shape the landscape to this day. As the river eroded the softer rock, it caused the falls to slowly retreat upstream, moving from their original location near what is now the Niagara Escarpment, a prominent geological feature that stretches across the region. The falls have moved approximately seven miles (11 kilometers) upstream from their original position over the course of thousands of years, and they continue to move backward due to the ongoing erosion of the underlying rock.

As the water flowed over the cliffs and eroded the rock below, the Niagara River eventually split into three separate waterfalls: Horseshoe Falls, American Falls, and Bridal Veil Falls. The most famous and powerful of these is Horseshoe Falls, named for its distinctive horseshoe-shaped curve. Horseshoe Falls formed as the river's flow became concentrated in one main channel, creating a massive waterfall that now straddles the border between the United States and Canada. This waterfall is the largest of the three, measuring approximately 2,700 feet wide and 167 feet tall, and it carries about 90% of the Niagara River's water flow.

The American Falls and Bridal Veil Falls, both located entirely on the U.S. side of the border, formed in a similar manner but are smaller and less powerful than Horseshoe Falls. The American Falls is approximately 940 feet wide and 100 feet tall, and it has a more rugged appearance, with large boulders at its base that have fallen from the cliffs above due to erosion. Bridal Veil Falls, the smallest of the three, is located to the right of the American Falls and is separated from it by a small island known as Luna Island. While these falls are smaller, they still play a significant role in the overall spectacle of Niagara Falls, contributing to the unique beauty and diversity of the landscape.

The formation of Niagara Falls is also deeply connected to the concept of "recession," which refers to the gradual retreat of the falls over time. The force of the water eroding the rock beneath the falls causes the waterfall to slowly move backward, a process that has been occurring for thousands of years. The falls have receded at an average rate of about one foot per year, although this rate has varied throughout history due to changes in water flow and other environmental factors. At times, the rate of recession has been much faster, especially during periods when the water flow was higher due to natural events such as floods or increased glacier melt.

One of the most dramatic examples of the falls' recession occurred around 11,000 years ago, when the falls were located near what is now the present-day town of Lewiston, New York. At that time, the falls were about seven miles downstream from their current location, and the water flowed over a steep cliff known as the Niagara Escarpment. As the water continued to erode the softer rock beneath the escarpment, the falls gradually moved upstream, carving out the deep gorge that now forms the Niagara River's path. This retreat continued over the millennia, bringing the falls closer to their present-day location.

The rate of recession has been significantly slowed in recent years due to human intervention. In the early 20th century, engineers began to harness the power of Niagara Falls for hydroelectric energy, diverting a portion of the water from the river to power stations on both the American and Canadian sides of the falls. This diversion has reduced the volume of water flowing over the falls, which in turn has slowed the rate of erosion. Today, the flow of water over the falls is carefully regulated by international agreements between the United States and Canada, ensuring that both the natural beauty of the falls and their utility as a source of renewable energy are preserved.

The geology of the Niagara region is another crucial aspect of the falls' formation. The Niagara Escarpment, a long, steep slope formed by millions of years of erosion, plays a vital role in shaping the landscape around the falls. This escarpment, which stretches from New York State across Ontario and Michigan, is composed of layers of limestone, dolomite, and shale. These layers of rock were deposited over 400 million years ago during the Silurian period, when the region was covered by a shallow tropical sea. Over time, the sea retreated, and the exposed rock layers were subject to the forces of erosion, creating the steep cliffs and dramatic landscapes that characterize the Niagara region today.

The interplay between the hard and soft rock layers is what makes Niagara Falls so dynamic. The harder dolomite rock on top is more resistant to erosion, while the softer shale beneath erodes more easily, causing the dolomite to break and fall away, further shaping the falls. This process is not only responsible for the falls' formation but also contributes to their ongoing transformation, as the falls continue to retreat and the gorge continues to deepen.

Another important factor in the formation of Niagara Falls is the impact of glacial activity on the region's topography. During the last Ice Age, the movement of glaciers across the landscape dramatically altered the terrain, creating deep valleys, ridges, and depressions that would later become the Great Lakes and the Niagara River. As the glaciers advanced and retreated, they scraped away the surface of the land, leaving behind a mixture of rocky debris known as "glacial till." This material, combined with the melting ice, helped to shape the course of the Niagara River and the surrounding landscape, ultimately leading to the creation of Niagara Falls.

The flow of water over the falls has also been influenced by changes in the climate and the environment. During periods of higher precipitation or increased glacier melt, the volume of water flowing over the falls would have been significantly greater, resulting in more dramatic erosion and faster rates of recession. Conversely, during periods of drought or lower water levels, the rate of erosion would have slowed, allowing the falls to remain more stable. These natural fluctuations in water flow, combined with human interventions such as hydroelectric power generation, have played a role in shaping the falls' appearance and rate of change over time.

In addition to the geological and environmental factors, the formation of Niagara Falls has also been shaped by the cultural and historical significance of the region. Indigenous peoples, including the Seneca and Mohawk tribes, have long revered the falls as a sacred site, and they played a key role in the early history of the region. The name "Niagara" is believed to have originated from the Iroquoian word "Onguiaahra," which means "the strait" or "thunder of waters," reflecting the deep spiritual connection the Indigenous people had with the falls.

As European explorers and settlers arrived in the region, Niagara Falls became an important landmark and a symbol of the untamed beauty of the North American wilderness. Early explorers such as French priest Father Louis Hennepin, who first documented the falls in the 1600s, helped to spread word of Niagara's majesty to Europe, attracting adventurers, artists, and tourists from around the world. Over the centuries, Niagara Falls has become a destination for travelers, honeymooners, and thrill-seekers, all drawn by the falls' breathtaking beauty and the sense of awe inspired by its immense power.

The formation of Niagara Falls is a testament to the incredible forces of nature that continue to shape the Earth. From the retreat of glaciers at the end of the Ice Age to the ongoing erosion of rock layers by the mighty Niagara River, the creation of this natural wonder is a story of transformation, resilience, and the enduring power of water.

Today, Niagara Falls stands not only as a marvel of geological history but also as a symbol of the delicate balance between human activity and the preservation of our planet's most precious natural resources. As the falls continue to evolve and change, they remind us of the dynamic, ever-shifting nature of the world around us.

Chapter 3: The Great Gorge Adventure

The Great Gorge Adventure is a journey into one of the most remarkable and awe-inspiring natural wonders in North America: the Niagara Gorge. Spanning over seven miles, the Niagara Gorge is a deep and majestic canyon carved by the relentless force of the Niagara River over thousands of years. The Gorge offers a breathtaking landscape of steep cliffs, rugged rock formations, thundering rapids, and lush vegetation, creating an environment that has both geological and historical significance. The Great Gorge Adventure is not just a trip through nature; it's an exploration of the powerful forces that have shaped the landscape, the rich cultural history of the region, and the incredible biodiversity that calls this area home.

The Niagara Gorge is located downstream from Niagara Falls, extending from the base of the American and Horseshoe Falls all the way to the Niagara Escarpment, a steep, rocky ridge that stretches across the region. The adventure begins at the brink of Niagara Falls, where the mighty Niagara River plunges over the falls, creating one of the most powerful and iconic waterfalls in the world. As the water crashes down, it continues its journey through the Niagara River Gorge, churning and swirling as it makes its way downstream. The journey through the gorge takes adventurers on a path through history, geology, and nature, offering a deeper understanding of the forces that have shaped this incredible landscape.

The story of the Niagara Gorge begins over 12,000 years ago, at the end of the last Ice Age. As the glaciers covering North America began to melt, massive amounts of water were released, carving out the Great Lakes and the Niagara River. The force of the water flowing from Lake Erie to Lake Ontario created the waterfalls that we now know as Niagara Falls. Over time, the powerful flow of the Niagara River eroded the softer rock layers beneath the harder dolomite caprock, creating the steep cliffs and deep canyon that form the Niagara Gorge.

This process, known as recession, has caused the falls to gradually move upstream over thousands of years, leaving the gorge in its wake.

The Great Gorge Adventure takes visitors into this ancient canyon, where they can witness the raw power of the river and the forces of erosion firsthand. One of the most popular ways to experience the gorge is by hiking along the many trails that wind through the canyon. These trails offer a unique opportunity to explore the natural beauty of the gorge, with stunning views of the river, the cliffs, and the surrounding forest. The most famous of these trails is the Niagara Gorge Trail, a series of pathways that run along the edge of the gorge and provide access to some of the most scenic and dramatic viewpoints in the area. Hikers can descend into the gorge itself, walking along the river's edge and feeling the mist from the rapids as the water rushes past.

As adventurers make their way along the trails, they will encounter a variety of geological formations that tell the story of the gorge's creation. The cliffs of the gorge are composed of layers of rock that were formed over millions of years, during a time when the region was covered by a shallow sea. These layers include limestone, dolomite, and shale, each with its own unique properties. The harder dolomite layer forms the caprock that sits on top of the gorge, while the softer shale layers beneath have been eroded by the river's flow, causing the cliffs to crack and collapse over time. This process of erosion continues to this day, with the falls slowly moving upstream and the gorge growing deeper and wider.

One of the most dramatic features of the Niagara Gorge is the Whirlpool, a giant, swirling pool of water located about two miles downstream from the falls. The Whirlpool was created by the force of the river as it makes a sharp turn, causing the water to spin in a powerful vortex. This natural phenomenon is a testament to the immense power of the river and the incredible forces at work within the gorge. The Whirlpool is a popular destination for visitors to the gorge, who can view it from several vantage points along the trails or even take a boat ride through the rapids to experience the swirling waters up close.

In addition to its geological significance, the Niagara Gorge is also a place of great historical importance. For thousands of years, the region was home to various Indigenous peoples, including the Seneca, who considered the gorge and the falls to be sacred. The Seneca and other Iroquoian-speaking peoples believed that the falls were inhabited by powerful spirits and that the gorge was a place of great spiritual energy. They would often travel through the gorge on hunting and fishing expeditions, using the river as a source of food and transportation.

The arrival of European explorers in the 17th century marked the beginning of a new chapter in the history of the Niagara Gorge. Early explorers such as Father Louis Hennepin were awestruck by the majesty of the falls and the gorge, and they helped to spread word of this natural wonder to the rest of the world. Over time, the area became a popular destination for travelers and adventurers, who came to experience the beauty and power of the falls and the surrounding landscape. The construction of bridges, roads, and railways in the 19th century made the gorge more accessible to visitors, and it soon became a major tourist attraction.

One of the most famous historical events to take place in the Niagara Gorge was the construction of the Niagara River Suspension Bridge, which was completed in 1855. This engineering marvel spanned the gorge and connected the United States and Canada, allowing for the easy movement of people and goods between the two countries. The bridge was an important symbol of the growing relationship between the two nations, and it played a key role in the development of the region as a center of trade and tourism.

The Great Gorge Adventure also offers a chance to explore the rich biodiversity of the region. The gorge is home to a wide variety of plant and animal species, many of which are unique to the area. The steep cliffs and rocky terrain create a habitat for a range of wildlife, including birds, mammals, reptiles, and amphibians. Visitors to the gorge may encounter species such as the peregrine falcon, which nests in the cliffs, or the Eastern Massasauga rattlesnake, a rare and endangered species that makes its home in the rocky crevices of the gorge. The river itself is teeming with fish, including species such as smallmouth bass, trout, and salmon, which make the Niagara River one of the most popular fishing destinations in the region.

The flora of the Niagara Gorge is equally diverse, with a wide range of plant species adapted to the unique conditions of the canyon. The steep cliffs and rocky soil provide a challenging environment for plants, but many species have thrived in these conditions, creating a rich and varied ecosystem. Visitors to the gorge will encounter a mix of deciduous and coniferous trees, as well as a variety of wildflowers, shrubs, and ferns. In the spring and summer months, the gorge is alive with color, as the wildflowers bloom and the trees burst into leaf, creating a vibrant and lush landscape.

One of the most exciting aspects of the Great Gorge Adventure is the opportunity to experience the river's rapids up close. The Niagara River is famous for its fast-flowing water and turbulent rapids, which create a thrilling and exhilarating experience for those brave enough to venture onto the river. Several companies offer guided rafting and jet boat tours through the rapids, allowing visitors to feel the power of the river firsthand as they navigate the swirling waters. These tours are not for the faint of heart, as the rapids can be extremely challenging and dangerous, but for those seeking an adrenaline rush, they provide an unforgettable adventure.

For those who prefer a more leisurely experience, the Great Gorge Adventure also offers opportunities for birdwatching, photography, and nature walks. The gorge is a popular destination for birdwatchers, who come to spot species such as bald eagles, ospreys, and herons, as well as a variety of smaller songbirds. Photographers will find plenty of opportunities to capture stunning images of the cliffs, the river, and the wildlife, as well as the dramatic changes in light and shadow that occur throughout the day as the sun moves across the sky.

The Niagara Gorge is also a place of scientific interest, attracting researchers and geologists who come to study the unique geological formations and the ongoing process of erosion. The gorge provides a living laboratory for scientists to observe the forces of nature at work, and it offers valuable insights into the history of the Earth and the dynamic processes that continue to shape our planet. The Great Gorge Adventure is not just a journey into the past, but also a glimpse into the future, as the landscape continues to evolve and change over time.

The Great Gorge Adventure is more than just a walk through a canyon; it's an exploration of one of the most unique and awe-inspiring natural environments in the world. From the towering cliffs and swirling rapids to the rich history and diverse wildlife, the Niagara Gorge offers something for everyone. Whether you're an outdoor enthusiast looking for an adrenaline-pumping adventure, a nature lover eager to explore the region's biodiversity, or a history buff interested in the cultural significance of the area, the Great Gorge Adventure has something to offer. It's an experience that will leave you with a deeper appreciation for the power of nature, the beauty of the natural world, and the rich history of one of North America's most iconic landmarks.

Chapter 4: The Mighty Niagara River

The Mighty Niagara River is one of the most powerful and iconic waterways in North America, playing a crucial role in shaping the geography, history, and culture of the region it flows through. Stretching approximately 36 miles (58 kilometers) in length, the Niagara River forms part of the border between the United States and Canada, running between Lake Erie and Lake Ontario. What makes the Niagara River truly exceptional is not just its size but its immense volume and force, as it serves as the primary water outlet for the Great Lakes Basin. With an average flow rate of 85,000 cubic feet per second, the Niagara River carries more than 20% of the world's fresh water through its channels. It is a river that has carved deep gorges, created majestic waterfalls, and fueled the imagination and livelihoods of countless generations.

The Niagara River's journey begins at the eastern end of Lake Erie, where its waters flow out into the Niagara Strait. Almost immediately, the river encounters a series of rapids and eddies as it courses toward the most famous natural feature along its path—Niagara Falls. This is where the true power of the river is on full display. As the river approaches the falls, it accelerates dramatically, surging over rocky outcrops and plunging more than 160 feet (50 meters) over the crest of the falls, creating a thunderous roar and a mesmerizing mist that has captivated visitors for centuries. The sight of the Niagara River cascading over the falls is one of the most iconic images in the natural world, drawing millions of tourists from around the globe every year.

The Niagara River's immense power is not confined to the spectacle of Niagara Falls. After the water tumbles over the brink of the falls, it continues its journey through the deep, narrow gorge that the river itself has carved over thousands of years. This stretch of the river, known as the Niagara Gorge, is one of the most geologically significant and dramatic landscapes in North America. The mighty force of the river has eroded the rock layers beneath it, cutting a path through the earth that is both steep and rugged. The gorge, with its towering cliffs and churning waters, provides a vivid demonstration of the erosive power of the river and its ability to shape the land over millennia.

The story of the Niagara River and its relationship with the land goes back more than 12,000 years, to the end of the last Ice Age. At that time, glaciers covered much of North America, and as they began to melt, they released vast quantities of water, forming the Great Lakes. The Niagara River was born from this process as the water from Lake Erie sought an outlet to the lower-lying Lake Ontario. Over time, the river began to erode the softer rock layers beneath it, carving out the Niagara Gorge and gradually retreating upstream, a process known as headward erosion. This process continues today, with the falls slowly moving upstream at a rate of about one foot per year.

While the geological power of the Niagara River is undeniable, it also holds tremendous historical and cultural significance. For thousands of years, the river was a vital resource for the Indigenous peoples who lived along its banks. The Seneca, a member of the Haudenosaunee (Iroquois) Confederacy, were among the many Native American groups who considered the river and the falls to be sacred. The river provided food, transportation, and spiritual nourishment for these communities, and it played a central role in their daily lives. The falls, in particular, were believed to be inhabited by powerful spirits, and the mist that rose from the base of the falls was seen as a direct connection to the spiritual world.

The arrival of European explorers in the 17th century marked the beginning of a new era in the history of the Niagara River. French explorer Samuel de Champlain and Jesuit missionary Father Louis Hennepin were among the first Europeans to document the river and the falls, and their accounts helped to spread word of this natural wonder to the rest of the world. Over the centuries that followed, the river became a key point of interest for settlers, traders, and soldiers.

During the War of 1812, the Niagara River played a strategic role as a border between British-controlled Canada and the United States, with several key battles fought along its shores.

In the 19th century, the Niagara River began to take on new significance as a center for industry and tourism. With the advent of the Industrial Revolution, engineers and entrepreneurs began to realize the potential of the river's immense power to generate energy. The first hydroelectric power plant was built along the river in 1881, harnessing the force of the water to produce electricity. This was the beginning of a new era in which the river's natural power was tapped to fuel the growth of industry in both Canada and the United States. Today, the Niagara River is home to some of the largest hydroelectric power plants in the world, providing electricity to millions of people across the region.

The industrialization of the Niagara River brought both opportunities and challenges. While the river's power helped to spur economic growth and development, it also led to significant environmental changes. By the early 20th century, concerns were growing about the impact of industrial pollution on the river's water quality and the natural beauty of the falls. Factories and power plants along the river's banks were discharging waste directly into the water, threatening the health of the ecosystem and the communities that depended on it. In response, environmental activists and conservationists began to advocate for greater protections for the river and its surrounding landscapes. This led to the creation of Niagara Falls State Park in 1885, the first state park in the United States, and the establishment of the Niagara Parks Commission in Canada.

The efforts to protect the Niagara River and its surrounding environment have had a lasting impact, and today the river is recognized not only for its natural beauty and power but also for its ecological importance. The Niagara River serves as a critical habitat for a wide range of plant and animal species, many of which are unique to the region. The river is home to numerous fish species, including salmon, trout, and bass, making it a popular destination for anglers. The surrounding forests and wetlands provide habitat for a variety of bird species, including peregrine falcons, bald eagles, and herons, as well as mammals such as deer, foxes, and beavers.

One of the most unique aspects of the Niagara River is its role as an international border. The river forms the natural boundary between the United States and Canada, and this has led to a rich and complex history of cooperation and conflict between the two nations. The Peace Bridge, which spans the river between Buffalo, New York, and Fort Erie, Ontario, is one of the busiest border crossings in North America, facilitating the movement of goods and people between the two countries. Over the years, the river has been a symbol of both division and unity, serving as a reminder of the shared natural heritage of the United States and Canada.

The Niagara River is also a place of great cultural and recreational significance. In addition to the millions of tourists who visit Niagara Falls each year, the river attracts outdoor enthusiasts from around the world. Boating, kayaking, and fishing are popular activities along the river, with many marinas and boat launches providing access to the water. The river's fast-moving currents and rapids offer thrilling experiences for white-water rafting and jet boating, while its calmer sections provide opportunities for leisurely paddling and wildlife observation. Hiking and biking trails along the riverbanks allow visitors to explore the natural beauty of the region, with stunning views of the river, the falls, and the surrounding landscape.

Despite its industrial and recreational uses, the Niagara River remains a vital natural resource, providing clean drinking water to millions of people in both the United States and Canada. The river's water is also used for agricultural irrigation, supporting the farming communities in the region. As concerns about climate change and water scarcity grow, the importance of protecting the Niagara River and ensuring its sustainability for future generations becomes even more critical.

In recent years, there have been significant efforts to restore and protect the Niagara River's ecosystem. Environmental organizations and government agencies on both sides of the border have worked to reduce pollution, restore natural habitats, and improve water quality in the river. These efforts have led to the return of several species of fish and wildlife that had previously been endangered or extinct in the region. The Niagara River is now recognized as a globally significant area for bird conservation, and it has been designated as a Ramsar Wetland of International Importance, highlighting its ecological value on a global scale.

The Niagara River is a living symbol of the power and beauty of nature. It has shaped the landscape, inspired countless generations, and played a central role in the development of the region. From its geological origins to its cultural and historical significance, the river tells the story of the dynamic relationship between humans and the natural world. Whether it's the roar of the falls, the rush of the rapids, or the tranquility of its quieter stretches, the Niagara River continues to captivate all who experience its majesty. It is a reminder of the forces that have shaped our planet and the need to protect and preserve these natural wonders for future generations to enjoy.

Chapter 5: Powering Up with Hydroelectricity

Powering up with hydroelectricity is an essential chapter in the story of human progress, particularly in relation to the utilization of natural resources for sustainable energy. Hydroelectric power, also known as hydroelectricity, refers to the process of generating electricity by harnessing the energy of moving water. Among the world's renewable energy sources, hydroelectricity stands out due to its reliability, efficiency, and low environmental impact compared to fossil fuels. This form of energy production has a long and fascinating history, and nowhere is it more evident than at places like Niagara Falls, where hydroelectric power has played a pivotal role in shaping modern industry, environmental conservation, and local economies.

The concept of using water to generate power is not new. Ancient civilizations such as the Greeks and Romans used water wheels to grind grain, saw wood, and perform other tasks that required mechanical energy. These early watermills were a precursor to modern hydroelectric power, as they demonstrated the potential of using water as a source of energy. However, the leap from mechanical energy to electrical energy occurred only in the late 19th century, during the industrial revolution, when scientists and engineers began exploring ways to convert kinetic energy from water into electricity.

The basic principle behind hydroelectricity lies in the conversion of the energy from moving water into electrical power. This process begins with a body of water, typically a river or reservoir, which is controlled by a dam or natural flow. As water flows downstream, it carries with it kinetic energy, which can be captured and directed toward turning turbines. When water is released from a higher elevation, it flows downward due to gravity, and the force of the moving water turns the blades of the turbines. The spinning of these turbines generates mechanical energy, which is then converted into electrical energy through generators connected to the turbines.

At the heart of any hydroelectric system is the dam, which plays a critical role in regulating water flow and creating the necessary pressure to drive the turbines. A dam essentially serves as a barrier, holding back water to form a reservoir. By controlling the release of water from this reservoir, engineers can ensure a steady and reliable supply of electricity. The higher the dam and the greater the volume of water, the more energy can be generated. The pressure created by the water behind the dam is known as the "head," and the higher the head, the more powerful the flow of water and the greater the amount of electricity that can be produced.

One of the most famous and iconic examples of hydroelectric power is found at Niagara Falls, where the force of the water has been harnessed for over a century to generate electricity. The falls, which straddle the border between the United States and Canada, have long been recognized for their potential to produce immense amounts of energy. The sheer volume of water that cascades over the falls every second—an average of more than 85,000 cubic feet—provides a nearly unlimited source of kinetic energy that can be converted into electricity. In fact, Niagara Falls is home to some of the oldest and most powerful hydroelectric plants in the world, and the area has become a symbol of the incredible potential of renewable energy.

The history of hydroelectric power at Niagara Falls dates back to the late 1800s when engineers began searching for ways to harness the energy of the falls for industrial use. In 1895, the first large-scale hydroelectric power plant, the Niagara Falls Power Company, was established on the American side of the falls. This pioneering project was the brainchild of businessman Edward Dean Adams and inventor George Westinghouse, who worked alongside the famous scientist Nikola Tesla to develop an innovative system for transmitting electricity over long distances using alternating current (AC) technology. Tesla's breakthrough made it possible to generate electricity at Niagara Falls and transmit it to Buffalo, New York, over 20 miles away, revolutionizing the way electricity was distributed and consumed.

The success of the Niagara Falls power plant marked the beginning of a new era in energy production and laid the groundwork for the widespread adoption of hydroelectric power. In the years that followed, additional power plants were built on both sides of the falls, increasing the region's capacity to generate electricity. Today, the Robert Moses Niagara Power Plant on the U.S. side and the Sir Adam Beck Hydroelectric Generating Stations on the Canadian side are two of the largest and most advanced hydroelectric facilities in North America. Together, these plants produce enough electricity to power millions of homes and businesses in the northeastern United States and southern Ontario.

Hydroelectric power is celebrated for its many advantages. One of its greatest strengths is its ability to provide a continuous and reliable source of electricity. Unlike solar or wind power, which can be intermittent due to changing weather conditions, hydroelectric power plants can operate around the clock, provided there is a consistent water supply. This makes hydroelectricity an ideal complement to other forms of renewable energy, as it can help stabilize the electrical grid and ensure a steady flow of power during times of high demand or low production from other sources.

Another major benefit of hydroelectricity is its low environmental impact. Unlike coal, oil, or natural gas, which release harmful greenhouse gases and pollutants into the atmosphere when burned, hydroelectric power generates electricity without emitting carbon dioxide or other pollutants. This makes it one of the cleanest forms of energy available, helping to reduce the overall carbon footprint of electricity generation. Furthermore, once a hydroelectric plant is built, the cost of operating and maintaining it is relatively low compared to other types of power plants, making it an economically viable and sustainable long-term solution for energy production.

In addition to providing clean energy, hydroelectric power plants can also offer other benefits to the surrounding environment and communities. Dams and reservoirs created for hydroelectric purposes can serve as valuable sources of water for drinking, irrigation, and recreation. Many reservoirs become popular destinations for boating, fishing, and swimming, contributing to local economies and providing recreational opportunities for residents and tourists alike. Dams also help control flooding by regulating the flow of water, preventing devastating floods that can damage homes, businesses, and infrastructure.

However, despite its many advantages, hydroelectric power is not without its challenges and controversies. One of the primary concerns associated with hydroelectric projects is the impact they can have on ecosystems and wildlife. The construction of dams and reservoirs can disrupt the natural flow of rivers, altering habitats for fish, plants, and animals. For example, fish that rely on migratory routes to spawn, such as salmon, may find their passage blocked by dams, leading to population declines. To mitigate these effects, many hydroelectric plants have implemented fish ladders or fish elevators, which allow fish to bypass the dams and continue their migration upstream.

Another concern is the displacement of communities and the loss of cultural heritage. Large-scale hydroelectric projects often require the flooding of vast areas of land to create reservoirs, which can lead to the displacement of people living in the affected areas. This has been a particular issue in regions such as China, where the construction of the massive Three Gorges Dam on the Yangtze River displaced more than a million people and submerged numerous towns and historical sites. The social and cultural costs of such projects must be carefully weighed against their potential benefits in terms of energy production and economic development.

In recent years, there has been a growing emphasis on developing smaller-scale hydroelectric projects that have less impact on the environment and local communities. These "run-of-the-river" systems generate electricity without the need for large dams or reservoirs, instead relying on the natural flow of the river to turn turbines. Run-of-the-river projects are considered to be more environmentally friendly, as they cause minimal disruption to river ecosystems and do not require the flooding of land. Additionally, advances in technology are allowing engineers to design more efficient turbines and generators, making it possible to extract more energy from smaller water sources.

The future of hydroelectric power looks promising as nations around the world continue to invest in renewable energy sources to combat climate change and reduce their reliance on fossil fuels. In countries like Norway, Iceland, and Brazil, hydroelectricity already accounts for the majority of the electricity supply, demonstrating the viability of this technology on a large scale. In other parts of the world, such as Africa and Southeast Asia, there is significant untapped potential for hydroelectric development, with many rivers and waterways that could be harnessed to provide clean, renewable energy to millions of people.

Hydroelectric power also plays an important role in energy storage. Pumped-storage hydroelectric plants, for example, can store energy by pumping water from a lower reservoir to an upper reservoir during times of low electricity demand. When demand increases, the stored water is released to generate electricity, providing a reliable and flexible source of power. This ability to store energy is especially important in the context of integrating variable renewable energy sources, such as wind and solar, into the electrical grid.

Despite these advancements, the future of hydroelectricity will require careful planning and consideration of environmental, social, and economic factors. As the global demand for clean energy continues to rise, balancing the benefits of hydroelectric power with the need to protect ecosystems and communities will be essential. Through innovative technology, sustainable practices, and responsible development, hydroelectric power can continue to be a cornerstone of the world's renewable energy future, providing a clean, reliable, and abundant source of electricity for generations to come.

In conclusion, powering up with hydroelectricity is not just a method of producing electricity; it represents a profound intersection of natural forces, human ingenuity, and the quest for a sustainable future. From its ancient origins to its modern-day applications, hydroelectric power has evolved into one of the most efficient and eco-friendly sources of energy available. Whether through massive dams like those at Niagara Falls or smaller, low-impact systems, hydroelectricity offers the potential to meet the world's growing energy needs while protecting the planet's natural resources. As we move forward in the 21st century, harnessing the power of water will continue to be an essential part of the global effort to transition to a cleaner, more sustainable energy future.

Chapter 6: Niagara Falls in History

Niagara Falls holds a unique and significant place in history, its captivating beauty and immense power having drawn explorers, settlers, scientists, industrialists, and travelers from all over the world for centuries. The story of Niagara Falls spans thousands of years, from its geological formation during the last ice age to its role in the development of industry, tourism, and international diplomacy. Throughout its history, the falls have served as a natural wonder, an industrial powerhouse, a contested borderland, and an inspiration for artists and adventurers alike.

Long before European settlers arrived, the area surrounding Niagara Falls was home to Indigenous peoples who had deep spiritual connections to the land and water. For the Iroquois Confederacy, particularly the Seneca and the Tuscarora Nations, the falls held immense cultural and religious significance. The Indigenous name for the falls, "Onguiaahra," meaning "the strait," reflected the geography of the region where the mighty Niagara River flowed between Lake Erie and Lake Ontario. The falls were considered a place of great power and mystery, and legends about the spirits of the falls were passed down through generations. One of the most famous Indigenous legends tells the story of Lelawala, a young woman who, in a tragic moment, went over the falls in a canoe and was saved by the Thunder God who lived behind the waterfall, granting her eternal life in the mist.

In the 17th century, European explorers began to make their way to North America, and reports of the majestic falls soon reached the ears of curious adventurers. The first recorded European to encounter Niagara Falls was the French explorer Samuel de Champlain, though he never actually saw the falls himself. It was Father Louis Hennepin, a French priest and explorer, who, in 1678, became the first European to describe the falls in detail after being taken to the site by Indigenous guides. Hennepin's account, published in his book *A New Discovery*, captured the imagination of Europeans and helped establish Niagara Falls as one of the natural wonders of the world. His description of the "vast and prodigious cadence of water" cascading from a great height intrigued readers and further fueled interest in the falls.

During the 18th century, the strategic importance of the Niagara region became apparent as European powers vied for control over the valuable fur trade and territorial claims in North America. The Niagara River, serving as a natural boundary between what would become Canada and the United States, was a key transportation route for Indigenous peoples and later for colonial settlers. Both the French and the British sought to establish military fortifications along the river to protect their interests. Fort Niagara, located near the mouth of the river on the U.S. side, and Fort George on the Canadian side, were both built in the early 1700s and became focal points in the conflict between the two colonial powers.

The Niagara Falls region played a crucial role during the American Revolutionary War and the War of 1812. Control over the area was seen as vital to the success of both British and American forces. The falls became a battleground, with numerous skirmishes and significant battles taking place nearby. One of the most famous engagements was the Battle of Lundy's Lane, fought in 1814, one of the bloodiest battles of the War of 1812. The outcome of this battle was indecisive, but it highlighted the strategic importance of the Niagara frontier. Throughout these conflicts, the falls themselves remained a symbol of the natural power that transcended human struggles, and the mist of Niagara bore witness to the ongoing drama of history.

As the 19th century unfolded, Niagara Falls began to take on a new role, transforming from a military frontier into a center of industrial development and a major tourist attraction. The Industrial Revolution brought new technologies and ideas about harnessing the natural power of the falls for industrial purposes. Engineers and entrepreneurs recognized the immense potential energy contained within the rushing waters of the Niagara River. Early attempts to harness this energy for mechanical use were modest, involving waterwheels to power mills and factories. However, by the mid-1800s, efforts were underway to utilize the falls for large-scale hydroelectric power generation, an endeavor that would ultimately revolutionize modern industry.

Tourism also began to flourish during this period, as improved transportation, including steamships and railways, made it easier for people to visit the falls. Niagara Falls became a premier destination for travelers from around the world, who were drawn by the opportunity to witness its natural grandeur firsthand. Prominent figures such as Charles Dickens, Mark Twain, and Frederick Douglass visited the falls, each leaving behind vivid descriptions of their experiences. The falls were often seen as a symbol of the sublime, embodying the raw and untamed forces of nature in an increasingly industrialized world. Romantic painters and poets captured the majesty of the falls in their works, further enhancing its reputation as a must-see natural wonder.

One of the most famous visitors to Niagara Falls in the 19th century was Annie Edson Taylor, who, in 1901, became the first person to survive going over the falls in a barrel. Taylor, a 63-year-old schoolteacher, undertook the dangerous stunt in hopes of achieving fame and fortune. Her successful descent over the falls marked the beginning of a long tradition of daredevils attempting to conquer Niagara's mighty waters. Over the years, numerous individuals have tried, with varying degrees of success, to navigate the falls in barrels, boats, and even tightropes. These daring feats have added to the mystique of Niagara Falls, attracting thrill-seekers and spectators alike.

While Niagara Falls became known for its spectacular scenery and daredevil stunts, it also became a focal point for technological innovation. In 1895, the world's first large-scale hydroelectric power plant was built at Niagara Falls, marking a turning point in the use of renewable energy. Pioneers like Nikola Tesla and George Westinghouse were instrumental in developing the alternating current (AC) system that made it possible to transmit electricity over long distances. Tesla's groundbreaking work at Niagara Falls helped usher in the modern era of electricity, as the energy generated by the falls powered homes and industries far beyond the immediate area. The success of hydroelectric power at Niagara Falls demonstrated the immense potential of renewable energy and set the stage for the widespread adoption of electricity across North America.

As the 20th century progressed, Niagara Falls continued to play a significant role in both tourism and industrial development. The falls became a symbol of international cooperation, particularly between the United States and Canada. The two countries worked together to manage the flow of the Niagara River, constructing dams and reservoirs to control water levels and prevent erosion of the falls. This collaboration led to the creation of the Niagara River Water Diversion Treaty in 1950, which formalized the management of the river for both power generation and the preservation of the falls as a natural wonder.

The construction of the Robert Moses Niagara Power Plant on the U.S. side and the Sir Adam Beck Hydroelectric Generating Stations on the Canadian side further solidified Niagara's role as a major source of renewable energy. Today, these power plants generate enough electricity to supply millions of homes and businesses in the surrounding regions, making Niagara Falls a critical component of North America's energy infrastructure. The falls' power has become a symbol of the balance between harnessing natural resources for human use while also preserving the environment for future generations.

Niagara Falls has also played an important role in environmental conservation. In the early 20th century, concerns about the impact of industrial development on the falls and the surrounding environment led to the establishment of the Niagara Falls State Park, the oldest state park in the United States. Spearheaded by landscape architect Frederick Law Olmsted, the park was designed to protect the natural beauty of the falls while providing public access to this magnificent landmark. The creation of the park marked an early example of the conservation movement in North America, highlighting the importance of preserving natural wonders for future generations.

In the latter half of the 20th century, Niagara Falls became a site of international diplomacy and environmental activism. In the 1960s, concerns about pollution in the Niagara River, particularly from industrial waste, led to efforts to clean up the river and protect the water quality of the Great Lakes. The Love Canal environmental disaster, which occurred near Niagara Falls in the 1970s, brought national attention to the dangers of toxic waste disposal and helped spur the development of environmental regulations in the United States and Canada.

Today, Niagara Falls continues to be a place where history, technology, and nature intersect. It remains one of the most popular tourist destinations in the world, drawing millions of visitors each year who come to experience its breathtaking beauty and learn about its rich history. The falls are a testament to the power of nature and the ingenuity of human beings, a place where the forces of the natural world have been harnessed to create energy, inspire art, and foster international cooperation. From its early beginnings as a sacred site for Indigenous peoples to its role in the development of modern industry and renewable energy, Niagara Falls has been a constant presence in the unfolding story of North America.

As we look to the future, Niagara Falls will continue to be a symbol of the delicate balance between progress and preservation. The ongoing efforts to protect the falls and the surrounding environment reflect a broader global movement toward sustainability and responsible stewardship of natural resources. At the same time, the falls remain a place of wonder and inspiration, a reminder of the awe-inspiring beauty and power of the natural world. Whether as a source of energy, a site of historical significance, or a beloved natural wonder, Niagara Falls will continue to hold a special place in the hearts and minds of people around the world for generations to come.

34

Chapter 7: The Daredevils of Niagara Falls

Niagara Falls, with its thundering waters and breathtaking beauty, has long captivated the imaginations of people worldwide. Its raw power, however, has also drawn a certain type of individual—those with an insatiable appetite for danger and an unquenchable thirst for fame. Throughout history, daredevils have been attracted to Niagara Falls like moths to a flame, risking their lives to perform incredible and often terrifying feats. These audacious individuals have attempted to conquer the falls in a variety of ways: plunging over them in barrels, walking across them on tightropes, or braving the treacherous rapids in makeshift vessels. While some succeeded and achieved instant celebrity status, others tragically lost their lives in their quests for glory. The legacy of the daredevils of Niagara Falls is filled with tales of courage, foolhardiness, and the irresistible lure of the mighty waterfall.

The history of daredevils at Niagara Falls begins in the early 19th century, as the falls became a prominent tourist destination. It didn't take long for the idea of challenging the natural wonder to arise in the minds of thrill-seekers. The first recorded daredevil stunt at Niagara Falls occurred in 1829, when a man named Sam Patch, known as the "Yankee Leaper," performed a daring jump from a platform near the base of the falls. Patch had gained fame for his death-defying jumps from bridges and cliffs, but his leap at Niagara was particularly dangerous due to the force of the water and the jagged rocks below. In front of a crowd of thousands, Patch successfully made his jump, landing safely in the swirling waters below. His feat not only earned him widespread acclaim but also set the stage for a long tradition of daredevils attempting to conquer the falls in increasingly creative and risky ways.

As the 19th century progressed, daredevil stunts at Niagara Falls became more elaborate, with individuals attempting to navigate the falls in barrels or other makeshift contraptions. The most famous of these early daredevils was undoubtedly Annie Edson Taylor, who in 1901 became the first person to survive going over the falls in a barrel. Taylor, a 63-year-old schoolteacher from Michigan, sought to secure her financial future by attempting the dangerous stunt. She had a custom-made barrel constructed out of oak and iron, padded with a mattress to help cushion her fall. On October 24, 1901, Taylor climbed into her barrel and was set adrift in the Niagara River, tumbling over the Horseshoe Falls. Miraculously, she survived the drop with only minor injuries, emerging from her barrel dazed but alive. Taylor's success made her an instant celebrity, and she traveled the country telling her story and displaying her barrel. However, despite her bravery, Taylor did not achieve the financial security she had hoped for, and she spent the rest of her life in relative obscurity.

Annie Edson Taylor's successful plunge over the falls inspired many others to follow in her footsteps, though not all were as fortunate. In the years following Taylor's historic feat, a number of individuals attempted to go over the falls in barrels, with varying degrees of success. One of the most famous of these daredevils was Bobby Leach, an English stuntman who became the second person to survive going over Niagara Falls in 1911. Leach, who had previously performed dangerous stunts in circuses, descended the falls in a steel barrel. Although he survived the fall, he was severely injured, suffering broken bones and a lengthy recovery. Nevertheless, Leach capitalized on his fame by touring the world and sharing his story. His luck ran out years later, however, when he slipped on an orange peel while on tour in New Zealand, suffering a leg injury that led to gangrene and ultimately his death.

In addition to barrel plunges, Niagara Falls also became the site of daring tightrope walks, another popular and perilous stunt. The most famous of these tightrope walkers was Jean François Gravelet, better known by his stage name, The Great Blondin. A French acrobat and aerialist, Blondin first crossed the Niagara Gorge on a tightrope in 1859, thrilling spectators with his astonishing balance and nerve. His initial crossing was just the beginning of a series of increasingly dangerous stunts. Blondin crossed the gorge multiple times, often performing daring feats along the way, such as crossing blindfolded, on stilts, or carrying his manager on his back. Perhaps his most famous stunt involved walking across the tightrope while pushing a wheelbarrow and stopping midway to cook an omelet on a portable stove. Blondin's incredible skill and showmanship earned him international fame, and he became a living legend in the world of daredevils. Unlike many of his contemporaries, Blondin lived to a ripe old age, dying of natural causes in 1897.

While Blondin's tightrope walks captured the public's imagination, he was not the only daredevil to attempt such feats at Niagara Falls. In the early 20th century, Italian-born aerialist Maria Spelterini became the first woman to cross the Niagara Gorge on a tightrope. Spelterini, like Blondin, performed a series of remarkable stunts during her crossings, including walking with her feet in baskets and with her arms and legs shackled. Spelterini's daring performances added to the growing tradition of tightrope walkers testing their skills against the awe-inspiring backdrop of Niagara Falls.

As the 20th century progressed, daredevils continued to push the limits of what was possible at Niagara Falls, often with disastrous results. While some, like Taylor and Leach, survived their stunts, many others met tragic fates. The immense power of the falls, combined with the unpredictability of the water and the jagged rocks below, made any attempt to conquer the falls a dangerous gamble. One of the most tragic examples was Charles Stephens, a barber from England who attempted to go over the falls in a barrel in 1920. Stephens had a barrel specially constructed for the stunt, but tragically, it was poorly designed. When Stephens went over the falls, the force of the water ripped him from the barrel, and only his right arm was found still strapped inside the wreckage. His death served as a sobering reminder of the risks involved in such dangerous feats.

Despite the dangers, the allure of Niagara Falls continued to draw daredevils throughout the 20th century and into the 21st. In 1984, Canadian daredevil Karel Soucek successfully went over the falls in a specially designed capsule, surviving with only minor injuries. Soucek's stunt garnered significant attention, but tragically, he was killed the following year during a similar stunt at the Houston Astrodome when his capsule malfunctioned during a drop from a height.

In more recent years, modern daredevils have taken on Niagara Falls with the help of advanced technology and equipment. In 2012, Nik Wallenda, a member of the famous Flying Wallendas circus family, became the first person in more than a century to walk a tightrope across the falls. Wallenda's walk was broadcast live on television, and millions of viewers around the world watched in awe as he crossed the 1,800-foot span over the Horseshoe Falls, battling wind, mist, and the deafening roar of the water below. Wallenda's successful crossing was a testament to the enduring fascination with Niagara Falls as a site of daredevilry and human achievement.

While stunts like Wallenda's have captured the attention of the public, there has also been increasing concern about the safety and environmental impact of daredevil stunts at Niagara Falls. In the 20th century, both the U.S. and Canadian governments implemented stricter regulations regarding stunts at the falls, in an effort to protect both the daredevils themselves and the natural environment. Today, anyone wishing to perform a stunt at Niagara Falls must obtain special permission from both countries, and safety protocols have been significantly strengthened to prevent accidents.

The legacy of the daredevils of Niagara Falls is one of incredible bravery, ingenuity, and, at times, tragic consequences. For many, the falls represent the ultimate challenge—an untamed natural force that beckons to those with a thirst for adventure and a desire to defy the odds. While some daredevils have achieved fame and fortune through their daring feats, others have paid the ultimate price in their pursuit of glory. The stories of these individuals, from Annie Edson Taylor to Nik Wallenda, are woven into the rich history of Niagara Falls, a place where nature's power and human courage collide.

Beyond the spectacle of the stunts themselves, the daredevils of Niagara Falls have also contributed to the mystique and allure of the falls as a global destination. Their incredible feats have drawn millions of spectators to the falls over the years, helping to establish Niagara as a symbol of both natural beauty and human tenacity. The daredevils, with their audacious attempts to conquer the falls, have become part of the enduring legacy of Niagara, a reminder of the lengths to which people will go to achieve fame, fortune, or simply the thrill of defying one of nature's most awe-inspiring wonders.

In conclusion, the daredevils of Niagara Falls have left an indelible mark on the history and culture of this iconic natural wonder. Their stories of bravery, ingenuity, and often tragedy have captivated the world for over a century, making Niagara Falls a site not only of natural beauty but also of human daring. From the early barrel riders to modern-day tightrope walkers, the daredevils of Niagara Falls embody the spirit of adventure and the timeless desire to push the boundaries of what is possible.

Chapter 8: Wildlife Around Niagara Falls

Niagara Falls is not only renowned for its stunning beauty and powerful waters, but also for the diverse and fascinating array of wildlife that inhabits the surrounding areas. Nestled between Canada and the United States, the falls are located within a unique ecosystem that provides a variety of habitats for animals, birds, and aquatic life. The region's rich biodiversity can be attributed to the abundance of natural resources, including freshwater, forests, wetlands, and grasslands. These environments create a sanctuary for both native and migratory species, making Niagara Falls a hotspot for nature enthusiasts and wildlife observers alike.

One of the most striking aspects of wildlife around Niagara Falls is the sheer number of bird species that call the area home. The falls lie along the Atlantic Flyway, one of the major migration routes for birds traveling between North and South America. Every year, thousands of birds pass through the region, stopping to rest and feed in the lush forests and along the banks of the Niagara River. Birdwatchers flock to Niagara Falls to witness this spectacular migration, with many species putting on a breathtaking display as they soar above the misty falls.

The diversity of bird species is astounding, ranging from small songbirds to larger raptors and waterfowl. One of the most notable birds in the area is the peregrine falcon, a bird of prey known for its incredible speed and hunting prowess. Peregrine falcons were once on the brink of extinction due to the widespread use of pesticides like DDT, but thanks to conservation efforts, their population has rebounded. The steep cliffs around Niagara Falls provide the perfect nesting sites for these falcons, and visitors to the falls can often catch a glimpse of them as they dive at astonishing speeds to catch their prey.

In addition to the peregrine falcon, the Niagara region is home to a variety of other birds of prey, including bald eagles, red-tailed hawks, and osprey. The bald eagle, a symbol of strength and freedom, is particularly revered by birdwatchers. These majestic birds can often be seen perched in tall trees along the river, scanning the water below for fish. Their impressive wingspan and striking white heads make them a sight to behold as they soar high above the falls. Ospreys, known as "fish hawks," are also a common sight in the area, diving dramatically into the river to snatch fish with their sharp talons.

Waterfowl are another prominent group of birds around Niagara Falls. Species such as mallards, Canada geese, and common mergansers thrive in the rivers and wetlands that surround the falls. Canada geese, with their characteristic honking calls, are a common sight in the region, especially during their seasonal migrations. These geese are known for their remarkable navigation skills, often traveling in V-shaped formations as they journey to their wintering or breeding grounds. Common mergansers, on the other hand, are expert divers, using their serrated bills to catch fish beneath the water's surface. They are often spotted gliding along the river in search of their next meal.

Niagara Falls is also home to a wide range of smaller bird species, including warblers, sparrows, and finches. During the spring and fall migrations, the forests and meadows around the falls come alive with the vibrant colors and melodic songs of these birds. Warblers, in particular, are known for their striking plumage and energetic behavior, flitting from branch to branch in search of insects. Their presence adds to the natural beauty of the area, as their bright feathers stand out against the lush greenery.

While the birdlife around Niagara Falls is certainly impressive, the region's wildlife is not limited to avian species. The surrounding forests, wetlands, and meadows provide a habitat for a variety of mammals, many of which are well adapted to the region's changing seasons. White-tailed deer are among the most common mammals in the area.

These graceful creatures can often be seen foraging in the meadows and forests that line the Niagara River. During the warmer months, they graze on grasses and shrubs, while in the winter, they rely on the buds and twigs of trees to sustain them. White-tailed deer are known for their distinctive tail, which they raise like a flag when alarmed, signaling danger to other deer in the area.

Another notable mammal found in the Niagara region is the beaver, North America's largest rodent. Beavers are famous for their ability to build dams, creating ponds and wetlands that provide crucial habitats for other wildlife. Along the quieter sections of the Niagara River and its tributaries, beavers can be seen hard at work, felling trees with their strong, sharp teeth and using the logs to construct their intricate dams and lodges. These industrious animals play a vital role in maintaining the health of the ecosystem, as their dams help regulate water flow and create rich wetlands that support a variety of species.

Raccoons are another common sight around Niagara Falls, especially in the evenings when they emerge from their hiding places to forage for food. These nocturnal mammals are highly adaptable and are known for their dexterous front paws, which they use to open containers, manipulate objects, and find food. Raccoons are opportunistic feeders, meaning they will eat almost anything they can find, from fruits and insects to small animals and even human leftovers. Despite their sometimes mischievous behavior, raccoons are an important part of the ecosystem, helping to control insect populations and clean up organic waste.

Smaller mammals, such as squirrels, chipmunks, and rabbits, are also common in the forests and fields around Niagara Falls. Eastern gray squirrels, with their bushy tails and acrobatic abilities, can often be seen scampering up and down trees, gathering nuts and seeds for the winter months. Chipmunks, on the other hand, are known for their distinctive stripes and their habit of storing food in their cheek pouches, which they later stash in underground burrows. These small but resourceful mammals play a key role in seed dispersal, helping to maintain the health of the forest ecosystem.

In addition to mammals and birds, the waters of Niagara Falls and the Niagara River are teeming with aquatic life. The river is home to a variety of fish species, including bass, trout, walleye, and muskellunge. The fast-flowing waters of the falls and the surrounding rapids provide an ideal environment for fish that are adapted to strong currents. One of the most well-known fish species in the region is the lake sturgeon, a prehistoric-looking fish that has been around for over 100 million years. Lake sturgeons can grow to impressive lengths, with some individuals reaching over six feet long. These bottom-dwelling fish are known for their distinctive bony plates and long, whisker-like barbels, which they use to sense food along the riverbed.

The Niagara River is also home to a variety of amphibians and reptiles, including frogs, turtles, and snakes. Painted turtles, with their bright yellow and red markings, can often be seen basking on rocks and logs near the water's edge, soaking up the sun. These turtles are well adapted to both aquatic and terrestrial environments, making their homes in the slow-moving sections of the river and the nearby wetlands. Northern water snakes, though non-venomous, are often mistaken for more dangerous species due to their size and aggressive behavior when threatened. These snakes are excellent swimmers and spend much of their time hunting for fish and amphibians in the river.

The wetlands and marshes surrounding Niagara Falls also provide crucial habitats for amphibians such as frogs and salamanders. These areas, rich in vegetation and shallow water, offer the perfect conditions for these creatures to breed and find food. Frogs, with their distinctive croaking calls, are a common sound in the evenings, as they gather near ponds and streams to attract mates. Salamanders, on the other hand, are more elusive and often remain hidden beneath logs or in damp soil during the day. Both frogs and salamanders play important roles in controlling insect populations, acting as natural pest controllers.

Beyond the terrestrial and aquatic animals, the plant life around Niagara Falls is equally diverse and vital to supporting the local wildlife. The region's forests are dominated by species such as maple, oak, and pine, which provide food and shelter for a wide range of animals. In the spring and summer months, the forests burst into life, with wildflowers blooming and trees providing a lush canopy of green. The meadows around the falls are also home to a variety of grasses and wildflowers, which attract pollinators such as bees, butterflies, and hummingbirds.

In addition to providing essential habitats for wildlife, the plant life around Niagara Falls plays a crucial role in stabilizing the soil and preventing erosion. The powerful waters of the falls and the river can cause significant erosion over time, but the roots of trees and other plants help to anchor the soil in place, reducing the impact of this natural process. Wetland plants, such as cattails and rushes, also help to filter and purify the water, ensuring that the ecosystem remains healthy and sustainable for both wildlife and humans.

As one of the most iconic natural wonders in North America, Niagara Falls is not just a breathtaking sight for visitors—it is also a thriving ecosystem that supports a diverse array of wildlife. From the majestic bald eagles and peregrine falcons that soar above the falls to the industrious beavers and elusive salamanders that inhabit the surrounding wetlands, the area is teeming with life. Each species, whether large or small, plays a vital role in maintaining the delicate balance of this ecosystem, contributing to the overall health and vitality of the region.

Efforts to conserve and protect the wildlife around Niagara Falls have become increasingly important in recent years. As human activities continue to impact natural habitats around the world, it is crucial to ensure that the unique ecosystems surrounding Niagara Falls are preserved for future generations. Conservation initiatives, such as habitat restoration projects and the protection of migratory bird routes, are helping to safeguard the biodiversity of the region, ensuring that Niagara Falls remains a sanctuary for wildlife for years to come.

In conclusion, the wildlife around Niagara Falls is as diverse and dynamic as the falls themselves. The region's unique blend of habitats, from forests and wetlands to rivers and cliffs, supports a wide range of species, each contributing to the rich tapestry of life that thrives in this natural wonderland. For nature lovers, birdwatchers, and wildlife enthusiasts, Niagara Falls offers an unparalleled opportunity to witness the beauty and complexity of the natural world in one of the most awe-inspiring settings on Earth.

Chapter 9: Exploring the Niagara Parks

Exploring Niagara Parks offers visitors a comprehensive journey through one of North America's most scenic and diverse regions. Spanning over 1,325 hectares along the Canadian side of the Niagara River, Niagara Parks is a mosaic of breathtaking natural beauty, historical landmarks, botanical gardens, recreational facilities, and conservation areas. It encapsulates much more than just the renowned Niagara Falls, offering year-round opportunities for education, exploration, and outdoor adventure. Whether you're fascinated by geology, intrigued by local history, or simply eager to experience the serene beauty of nature, Niagara Parks has something for everyone. As a natural, cultural, and historical treasure trove, it invites millions of visitors each year to delve deeper into the wonder that surrounds the famous falls and the park's many hidden gems.

A visit to Niagara Parks typically starts at the majestic Niagara Falls. As the focal point of the park, the falls themselves are awe-inspiring and draw countless tourists annually, who come to witness the raw power and beauty of the cascading waters. Comprising three separate falls—Horseshoe Falls, American Falls, and Bridal Veil Falls—this natural wonder is a defining feature of the park. The Horseshoe Falls, the largest of the three, is located on the Canadian side and plunges over 167 feet (51 meters) into the gorge below. Visitors can enjoy panoramic views of the falls from the many vantage points along the Niagara Parkway or experience them up close by boarding a boat tour like the famous Maid of the Mist or Hornblower Niagara Cruises. The falls' constant mist often creates stunning rainbows, further enhancing the magical ambiance of the park.

Beyond the falls themselves, Niagara Parks offers a multitude of ways to explore and engage with the natural world. One of the park's most notable attractions is the Niagara Glen Nature Reserve, a natural marvel situated deep in the Niagara Gorge. The Glen is renowned for its rugged hiking trails that wind through ancient forests, past towering limestone cliffs, and along the swirling waters of the Niagara River's rapids. The trails, which range from easy to challenging, provide hikers with an opportunity to explore one of the most significant geological formations in the region. The Niagara Glen is also home to a variety of plant and animal species, making it a haven for nature enthusiasts and wildlife watchers. In addition, the area is rich in fossils and unique rock formations, offering a glimpse into the geological history of the region, which dates back over 400 million years.

While the Glen attracts hikers and geology enthusiasts, Niagara Parks is also home to the Botanical Gardens, a lush 99-acre (40-hectare) sanctuary that features a wide variety of carefully cultivated plants, trees, and flowers. Established in 1936, the gardens are a testament to the park's commitment to conservation and environmental education. Visitors can stroll through themed gardens, including the world-famous Rose Garden, which boasts over 2,400 rose bushes, as well as a collection of perennial gardens, herbaceous borders, and formal flower beds. The gardens are meticulously maintained, offering a peaceful retreat for those seeking to immerse themselves in the beauty of nature. Adjacent to the Botanical Gardens is the Butterfly Conservatory, one of the park's most popular attractions. Home to over 2,000 free-flying butterflies from around the world, the conservatory offers an enchanting experience as visitors walk through a lush tropical rainforest environment while colorful butterflies flutter around them. It's a magical escape, especially for families and children, who delight in the opportunity to see butterflies up close.

Niagara Parks also serves as a living museum of local and national history. Historical landmarks dot the landscape, telling the story of the region's rich heritage. One of the most significant historical sites is the Old Fort Erie, a reconstructed military fort that played a pivotal role in the War of 1812 between the United States and Britain. Located on the shores of Lake Erie, the fort provides visitors with a glimpse into military life during the early 19th century. Interactive exhibits, guided tours, and live reenactments bring history to life as visitors learn about the strategic importance of the fort and the battles that took place there. The fort's grounds also serve as the final resting place for many soldiers who fought in the war, adding a somber and reflective dimension to the site.

Another historical gem within Niagara Parks is the Laura Secord Homestead, the restored home of Canadian heroine Laura Secord, whose brave journey during the War of 1812 helped alert British forces to an impending American attack. Visitors to the homestead can explore the beautifully restored 1812-era home and learn about Secord's daring 32-kilometer trek through wilderness to deliver her critical message, an act that cemented her legacy in Canadian history. The site offers a fascinating glimpse into the daily life of early Canadian settlers, with knowledgeable guides providing context and stories about Secord's life and the broader historical events of the time.

Niagara Parks is also home to several monuments and memorials that commemorate important historical events and figures. One such landmark is the Brock Monument, a towering column located in Queenston Heights Park, which honors Major General Sir Isaac Brock, a British military leader who played a key role in the defense of Upper Canada during the War of 1812. The monument, which stands 56 meters tall, is the focal point of Queenston Heights Park and offers visitors the chance to climb to the top for panoramic views of the surrounding landscape. The park itself is a popular spot for picnics and leisurely strolls, with beautifully landscaped gardens, historical plaques, and scenic overlooks.

For those interested in the agricultural heritage of the region, the McFarland House offers a unique window into Niagara's rich farming history. Built in 1800, the McFarland House is one of the oldest surviving structures in Niagara-on-the-Lake and provides insight into the early pioneer life of the area. Visitors can take guided tours of the house, which has been meticulously restored to reflect the period, and learn about the McFarland family's contributions to the local community, including their role in the early development of the area's agricultural industry. The house is surrounded by beautiful gardens and an apple orchard, further highlighting Niagara's long-standing connection to farming and agriculture.

In addition to its natural beauty and historical significance, Niagara Parks is also a hub for recreational activities. The Niagara River Recreation Trail, which stretches 56 kilometers from Fort Erie to Niagara-on-the-Lake, offers cyclists, walkers, and joggers a scenic route along the river, with stunning views of the Niagara Gorge, the river, and the surrounding landscape. The trail passes through numerous parks, historical sites, and natural attractions, making it an ideal way for visitors to explore the diverse offerings of Niagara Parks at their own pace. The park also offers opportunities for water-based activities, including boating, fishing, and kayaking along the calmer sections of the river. In the winter months, the park transforms into a snowy wonderland, with opportunities for cross-country skiing, snowshoeing, and ice skating at various locations.

Niagara Parks is also committed to environmental sustainability and conservation. The park's stewardship programs aim to protect and preserve the natural ecosystems within its boundaries while educating visitors about the importance of conservation. The Niagara Parks Commission, which manages the park, works closely with local organizations, governments, and conservation groups to ensure that the park's natural and cultural resources are protected for future generations. This commitment to sustainability is evident in the park's many green initiatives, including habitat restoration projects, invasive species management, and efforts to reduce the park's carbon footprint.

In recent years, Niagara Parks has also embraced eco-tourism, offering visitors opportunities to explore the park's natural wonders in an environmentally friendly way. Guided eco-tours provide in-depth information about the region's ecology, geology, and wildlife, allowing visitors to gain a deeper understanding of the natural world around them. These tours are designed to be educational and interactive, encouraging visitors to connect with nature and appreciate the importance of conservation.

For families, Niagara Parks offers a variety of kid-friendly attractions and activities that combine fun with education. Children can participate in interactive programs, nature walks, and hands-on exhibits that teach them about the region's wildlife, ecosystems, and history. The park's numerous playgrounds, picnic areas, and recreational facilities provide plenty of opportunities for family-friendly outdoor fun.

As one of Canada's premier travel destinations, Niagara Parks continues to evolve, offering new experiences while maintaining its commitment to preserving the natural and historical treasures that make it so special. Whether you're visiting for a day or planning an extended stay, Niagara Parks provides endless opportunities to explore, learn, and enjoy the beauty and history of this extraordinary region. From the thunderous roar of the falls to the quiet serenity of its forests and gardens, Niagara Parks offers a journey through time, nature, and culture that leaves a lasting impression on all who visit.

Chapter 10: The Mysteries of the Whirlpool Rapids

The Whirlpool Rapids of Niagara Falls is one of the most awe-inspiring and mysterious natural wonders associated with the falls. Located downstream of the famous Horseshoe Falls, this section of the Niagara River offers a dramatic display of nature's raw power, where the mighty river narrows and plunges through a gorge, creating some of the most treacherous and turbulent waters in North America. The rapids themselves are a result of the river's steep descent and narrow confines, producing currents that can reach speeds of up to 30 miles per hour (48 kilometers per hour). These rapids culminate in a whirlpool that has fascinated scientists, adventurers, and visitors alike for centuries.

The Whirlpool Rapids are formed as the Niagara River makes a sharp, almost 90-degree turn, forcing the water into a violent swirling motion. The sheer volume of water flowing through the gorge—an estimated 100,000 cubic feet per second—combined with the sudden change in direction creates powerful and chaotic whirlpools that seem to defy gravity and logic. The whirlpool is a large, bowl-shaped depression in the riverbed, and it is here that the water spins in a circular motion, creating a vortex that has long been shrouded in mystery and intrigue.

One of the most captivating aspects of the Whirlpool Rapids is the question of how this natural phenomenon came to be. The geological history of the Niagara region offers some clues, as the area has been shaped by glacial activity over thousands of years. During the last Ice Age, massive glaciers covered much of North America, and as they retreated, they left behind a landscape marked by deep gorges, steep cliffs, and fast-flowing rivers. The Niagara River, which was once much wider and slower, was gradually forced into its current path as the glaciers receded, carving out the narrow gorge through which the rapids now flow.

However, the precise formation of the whirlpool itself remains a topic of debate among geologists and hydrologists. Some believe that the whirlpool was created as a result of a sudden and catastrophic collapse of the riverbed, possibly caused by the weight of the glaciers or the intense pressure of the water. Others suggest that the whirlpool formed more gradually, as the river eroded the softer layers of rock beneath the surface over millennia. Whatever the exact cause, the result is a unique and powerful natural feature that has captivated the imagination of those who have witnessed it.

The Whirlpool Rapids have long been a source of fascination for scientists and researchers who seek to understand the dynamics of such extreme water currents. The rapids are categorized as Class VI whitewater, which is the highest level on the International Scale of River Difficulty. This means that the water is considered extremely dangerous, with unpredictable currents, massive waves, and powerful undertows. For centuries, the Whirlpool Rapids have been regarded as virtually unnavigable, and few have dared to attempt crossing them. Those who have tried often paid with their lives, as the rapids are unforgiving and leave little room for error.

Despite the dangers, the Whirlpool Rapids have also attracted a number of thrill-seekers and daredevils over the years. In the late 19th and early 20th centuries, a series of daring stunts were attempted in the rapids, with varying degrees of success. Perhaps the most famous of these daredevils was Charles Blondin, a French acrobat and tightrope walker who gained international fame by crossing the Niagara Gorge on a tightrope in 1859. While Blondin did not specifically target the Whirlpool Rapids, his stunts inspired others to take on the more dangerous sections of the river, including the rapids and the whirlpool itself.

One of the most notorious attempts to conquer the Whirlpool Rapids came in 1886, when Captain Matthew Webb, the first person to swim the English Channel, decided to take on the rapids. Webb, who was renowned for his endurance and strength as a swimmer, believed he could survive the treacherous waters and emerge victorious. Tragically, he was wrong. Webb entered the rapids and was almost immediately swept away by the powerful currents. His body was later found downstream, a stark reminder of the dangers posed by the Whirlpool Rapids.

In the decades that followed, a number of other daredevils attempted to navigate the rapids in various contraptions, including barrels, rubber rafts, and specially designed boats. Some succeeded in surviving the journey, while others met a grim fate. The unpredictability of the rapids, combined with the powerful whirlpool at the end, made each attempt a gamble with life and death. The whirlpool itself adds another layer of danger, as the swirling waters can trap anything that enters, pulling it into the vortex with incredible force. Even the strongest swimmers and most experienced boatmen can find themselves helpless against the whirlpool's relentless pull.

In addition to its physical dangers, the Whirlpool Rapids have also become a focal point for stories of mystery and legend. Over the years, numerous tales have emerged about strange occurrences and unexplained phenomena in the area. Some locals and visitors have reported seeing ghostly apparitions near the rapids, including the spirits of those who lost their lives attempting to navigate the treacherous waters. Others have claimed to hear eerie sounds, such as disembodied voices or the cries of the doomed, carried on the wind above the roar of the rapids. While these stories are likely the result of folklore and imagination, they add to the sense of mystery and intrigue that surrounds the Whirlpool Rapids.

The whirlpool itself has also been the subject of speculation and wonder. Some believe that the whirlpool has hidden depths, with underwater caves or channels that connect to other parts of the river or even to other bodies of water. While there is no scientific evidence to support these claims, the whirlpool's powerful currents and swirling waters make it difficult to explore fully. Modern technology, including sonar and underwater cameras, has allowed scientists to map parts of the whirlpool and study its behavior, but much of it remains unexplored and unknown.

In recent years, the Whirlpool Rapids have become a popular destination for tourists and adventurers who seek to experience the power and beauty of this natural wonder up close. The Whirlpool Aero Car, a cable car that has been in operation since 1916, offers visitors a bird's-eye view of the rapids and the whirlpool below. The Aero Car travels across the gorge, providing a unique perspective of the swirling waters and the dramatic landscape. For those who prefer to stay on solid ground, there are a number of hiking trails that lead to viewpoints along the Niagara Gorge, where visitors can watch the rapids from a safe distance.

In addition to its appeal as a natural spectacle, the Whirlpool Rapids also play an important role in the ecology of the Niagara River. The turbulent waters provide a habitat for a variety of fish species, including salmon and trout, which are able to navigate the rapids during their spawning migrations. The fast-moving water also helps to oxygenate the river, creating a healthy environment for aquatic life. In this way, the Whirlpool Rapids contribute to the overall health and biodiversity of the Niagara River ecosystem.

Today, the Whirlpool Rapids continue to captivate and challenge those who encounter them. Whether viewed from the safety of the Aero Car or from the rocky cliffs of the Niagara Gorge, the rapids offer a glimpse into the raw, untamed power of nature. For scientists, they present an ongoing mystery, as researchers continue to study the complex dynamics of the rapids and the whirlpool in an effort to better understand their formation and behavior. For thrill-seekers, the rapids remain a symbol of danger and adventure, a test of skill and courage for those daring enough to face them. And for visitors, the Whirlpool Rapids serve as a reminder of the beauty and power of the natural world, a place where the forces of water, rock, and time come together to create a spectacle unlike any other.

In the end, the mysteries of the Whirlpool Rapids may never be fully understood, and perhaps that is part of their enduring allure. As long as the Niagara River continues to flow, the rapids will remain a place of wonder, danger, and fascination—a reminder that even in the age of modern science and technology, there are still places where nature reigns supreme, and the mysteries of the natural world remain unsolved.

Chapter 11: The Legends of Niagara Falls

Niagara Falls, one of the most iconic natural wonders of the world, has captivated the imagination of people for centuries. Beyond its sheer beauty and immense power, the falls are also steeped in mystery, myth, and legend. Over the centuries, countless stories have been passed down through generations, each adding to the rich cultural tapestry surrounding the falls. These legends, which have been shaped by the native peoples, explorers, settlers, and travelers who have visited the falls, offer fascinating insights into how humans have interacted with this awe-inspiring natural phenomenon. The legends of Niagara Falls are as varied as they are compelling, and they range from tales of love and sacrifice to stories of supernatural occurrences and divine intervention.

One of the most enduring and poignant legends associated with Niagara Falls is that of the Maid of the Mist, a story that originates from the indigenous peoples of the region, particularly the Seneca and Iroquois nations. According to this ancient legend, a beautiful young woman named Lelawala, the daughter of a powerful chief, was deeply distraught after the death of her beloved husband. Overcome with grief, Lelawala chose to sacrifice herself to the great waters of Niagara in the hope of reuniting with her love in the afterlife. She climbed into a canoe and paddled out into the raging river, allowing the current to carry her toward the edge of the falls. As her canoe approached the brink, it is said that the powerful spirit of Hinu, the Thunder God who resided in a cave behind the falls, took pity on Lelawala and saved her from certain death. Hinu carried her to his realm, where she lived as his bride, becoming the spirit guardian of the falls.

The tale of the Maid of the Mist has been passed down through generations, and it continues to capture the imaginations of those who hear it. Over time, the legend has evolved and taken on different forms, but its central theme of sacrifice, love, and the mystical connection between humans and nature remains intact. The Maid of the Mist has also become a symbol of the falls themselves, and her name has been immortalized in the famous Maid of the Mist boat tours that take visitors on a thrilling journey to the base of the falls. For many, the legend of the Maid of the Mist serves as a reminder of the spiritual and emotional power that Niagara Falls holds over those who encounter it.

Another legendary tale from the Niagara region is the story of the Thunder Beings, powerful spirits believed to control the forces of nature, particularly thunder and lightning. According to Iroquois mythology, the Thunder Beings are ancient deities who reside in the sky and in the cave behind Niagara Falls, where they govern the weather and protect the natural world. It is said that the Thunder Beings use the falls as a gateway to travel between their world and the human realm, and that the sound of the thunderous waters crashing down is the voice of these spirits communicating with one another. The Thunder Beings are seen as both protectors and enforcers of natural balance, and they are said to punish those who disrespect the environment or disturb the sacred falls.

The legend of the Thunder Beings has been intertwined with the spiritual beliefs of the indigenous peoples of the Niagara region for centuries, and it continues to be an important part of their cultural heritage. The falls are viewed as a sacred site, where the powerful forces of nature are constantly at work, and the Thunder Beings serve as guardians of this sacred place. Many indigenous people still regard Niagara Falls with deep reverence, and they see the falls as a place of spiritual significance, where the boundary between the human world and the spirit world is blurred.

Another intriguing legend associated with Niagara Falls is the tale of Leaping Waters, a haunting love story that has been passed down through generations. According to this legend, a young Native American warrior named He-No fell in love with a beautiful maiden from a neighboring tribe. The two were deeply in love, but their relationship was forbidden due to a longstanding feud between their tribes. Unable to be together in life, He-No and his beloved made a pact to be united in death. One night, under the cover of darkness, they fled to the falls and leaped into the swirling waters together, choosing to end their lives rather than live apart. It is said that the spirit of He-No still inhabits the falls, watching over the waters and protecting those who visit the falls with pure hearts. Some believe that on quiet nights, the sound of his mournful cries can still be heard above the roar of the falls, a ghostly reminder of his undying love and tragic fate.

The supernatural allure of Niagara Falls is not limited to indigenous legends. Over the centuries, numerous tales of hauntings and paranormal occurrences have emerged from the region, further cementing its reputation as a place of mystery and intrigue. One of the most famous ghost stories associated with the falls is the tale of the Old Stone Chimney, a relic from the early European settlement of the area. The chimney is all that remains of an old French barracks that once stood near the falls, and it is said to be haunted by the spirits of soldiers who died there during the French and Indian War. Locals and visitors alike have reported seeing ghostly figures near the chimney, as well as hearing strange sounds, such as footsteps and whispers, in the dead of night. The Old Stone Chimney has become a popular destination for ghost hunters and paranormal enthusiasts, who are drawn to the eerie atmosphere and the lingering sense of history that surrounds it.

Another legend from the Niagara region involves the Devil's Hole, a treacherous and rocky gorge located just north of the falls. According to local lore, the Devil's Hole is home to an evil spirit that lures unsuspecting travelers to their doom. The legend dates back to the 18th century, when a group of British soldiers were ambushed by Native American warriors in the gorge during the Battle of Devil's Hole. The soldiers, who were transporting supplies along the portage road, were caught off guard and massacred by the warriors, who used the steep cliffs of the gorge to their advantage. The bloodshed was so intense that the waters of the Niagara River were said to have run red with the blood of the fallen soldiers. In the years that followed, stories began to circulate about a malevolent presence in the gorge, and many claimed that the Devil himself resided in the area. To this day, the Devil's Hole remains a place of fear and fascination, with some visitors reporting strange occurrences and an overwhelming sense of dread when they venture too close to the edge.

Legends of buried treasure also abound in the Niagara region, adding to the mystique of the falls. One of the most famous treasure legends involves the French explorer Louis Hennepin, who is credited with being the first European to document Niagara Falls in 1678. According to the legend, Hennepin and his crew discovered a hidden cache of gold and jewels near the falls, but they were forced to flee before they could retrieve the treasure. The treasure was supposedly buried somewhere along the banks of the Niagara River, and over the centuries, numerous treasure hunters have sought to uncover its location. While no one has ever found the fabled treasure, the legend persists, and the allure of hidden riches continues to draw adventurers to the area.

The legends of Niagara Falls extend beyond tales of love, loss, and treasure. There are also stories of miraculous survival and divine intervention associated with the falls. One such story is the legend of Annie Edson Taylor, the first person to go over the falls in a barrel and survive. In 1901, Taylor, a 63-year-old schoolteacher, decided to take the plunge in an effort to gain fame and fortune. She climbed into a custom-made barrel and was set adrift in the Niagara River, where she was carried over the edge of the falls and into the churning waters below. Miraculously, Taylor emerged from the barrel relatively unscathed, although she later described the experience as terrifying and painful. Taylor's daring feat became the stuff of legend, and she is still remembered today as one of the most famous daredevils to challenge the falls.

The sheer power and majesty of Niagara Falls have also inspired countless stories of divine intervention and religious significance. Some believe that the falls are a manifestation of a higher power, and that the natural beauty and strength of the falls are evidence of God's presence on Earth. Over the years, religious groups and spiritual leaders have made pilgrimages to the falls, seeking to connect with the divine through the awe-inspiring force of nature. The falls have been described as a place of healing and renewal, where visitors can experience a profound sense of peace and spiritual clarity.

In conclusion, the legends of Niagara Falls are as diverse and captivating as the falls themselves. From ancient indigenous myths to tales of daring explorers and supernatural hauntings, the falls have long been a source of wonder and inspiration for those who encounter them. These legends, whether rooted in fact or fiction, serve to deepen the mystique of Niagara Falls, reminding us that there is still much about this natural wonder that remains unknown. As long as the falls continue to flow, the stories and legends associated with them will endure, adding to the rich cultural heritage of this iconic landmark.

Chapter 12: Visiting the Falls in Winter

Visiting Niagara Falls in winter is like stepping into a magical, frozen wonderland where the thundering waterfalls transform into a serene yet powerful spectacle. While Niagara Falls is breathtaking year-round, the winter season adds a unique layer of beauty and tranquility to this world-famous destination. Covered in snow and ice, the entire area takes on an otherworldly charm, offering visitors a chance to experience the falls in a way that few people have ever seen. The combination of natural beauty, the crisp winter air, and the dramatic contrast between the icy stillness and the roaring water creates an unforgettable experience.

As the temperature drops, the mist from the falls freezes on nearby trees, railings, and pathways, creating a sparkling, frosty landscape that resembles a scene straight out of a winter fairy tale. Every surface glistens with ice, and icicles hang from branches and rocks, adding a sense of quiet elegance to the area. The most striking sight, however, is the falls themselves. While the water continues to flow, sections of the falls become encased in thick layers of ice, giving the illusion that the mighty Niagara River has frozen in time. Massive ice formations build up at the base of the falls, creating a frozen mountain of ice that adds to the dramatic scene.

One of the most magical aspects of visiting Niagara Falls in winter is seeing the Ice Bridge, a natural ice formation that stretches across the Niagara River below the falls. This occurs when the surface of the river freezes over, forming a solid sheet of ice that spans the width of the river. In the past, people would walk across the Ice Bridge, even setting up stalls and shops on its surface. However, due to safety concerns, walking on the Ice Bridge is no longer permitted. Still, it remains an awe-inspiring sight, as the river transforms into a vast expanse of ice, blending seamlessly with the snowy landscape.

For those who venture to the falls in winter, there are plenty of activities and attractions that make the visit worthwhile. The Niagara Falls Winter Festival of Lights, one of the most popular winter events in the region, turns the area into a dazzling display of holiday lights and decorations. From November through January, the festival illuminates the parkways and attractions around the falls with millions of sparkling lights, including illuminated displays, trees wrapped in twinkling lights, and festive decorations that add to the winter wonderland atmosphere. Visitors can take a leisurely drive or walk through the festival's light displays, which include glowing reindeer, snowflakes, and other winter-themed figures.

Another highlight of visiting Niagara Falls in winter is the opportunity to see the falls illuminated at night. Throughout the year, Niagara Falls is lit up by powerful spotlights that change colors, but in winter, the ice-covered falls take on an even more enchanting appearance when bathed in vibrant hues of blue, purple, red, and green. The ice and mist catch the light, creating a shimmering, iridescent effect that makes the falls look even more mystical. The nightly illumination is a must-see for any visitor, and it's especially magical during the winter months when the cold air and frosty surroundings heighten the sense of wonder.

The Journey Behind the Falls, one of the most popular attractions at Niagara Falls, takes on a special charm in winter. This attraction allows visitors to descend 150 feet via elevator to a series of tunnels that lead behind the falls. From there, visitors can view the icy cascades from observation decks that offer a unique perspective of the thundering water and frozen formations. In winter, the freezing mist creates a surreal environment, with ice forming on the railings and walkways, making the entire experience feel like a walk through an ice cave. Despite the cold, the Journey Behind the Falls is an unforgettable way to get up close to the powerful force of nature, even in the heart of winter.

For those who love outdoor activities, Niagara Falls offers a range of winter sports and recreation opportunities. One of the most popular activities is ice skating at the nearby Wayne Gretzky Estates Winery and Distillery, where visitors can glide across an outdoor rink surrounded by vineyards and winter landscapes. Additionally, snowshoeing and cross-country skiing are available in the surrounding parks, where trails wind through snow-covered forests and offer stunning views of the falls and the Niagara River. These activities provide a peaceful way to enjoy the natural beauty of the area while getting some fresh air and exercise.

Winter is also the perfect time to explore the Niagara Parks, which remain open year-round and offer plenty of opportunities for winter hiking and sightseeing. The Niagara Parks Botanical Gardens, which are lush and green in the warmer months, take on a serene, snow-covered beauty in winter. The gardens' towering trees and manicured landscapes are blanketed in snow, and the frozen ponds and sculptures make for a picturesque setting. Visitors can also explore the Butterfly Conservatory, which provides a warm, tropical escape from the cold. Inside, thousands of butterflies flutter among lush plants and flowers, offering a striking contrast to the icy conditions outside.

Another must-see winter attraction is the Niagara Glen Nature Reserve, a stunning area of rugged cliffs, rock formations, and pristine forests located just north of the falls. In winter, the glen is transformed into a snow-covered wilderness, and the trails become a peaceful haven for winter hikers and nature enthusiasts. The reserve offers breathtaking views of the Niagara River and the surrounding landscape, and the quiet, snowy surroundings make it feel like a hidden winter oasis. It's a great place to explore for those who want to experience the natural beauty of the region away from the crowds.

Visiting the falls in winter also offers a unique opportunity to see the Whirlpool Rapids in their frozen glory. Located downstream from the falls, the Whirlpool is a natural wonder where the Niagara River makes a sharp turn, creating a swirling, turbulent pool of water. In winter, the powerful rapids are often partially frozen, with chunks of ice swirling in the water, creating a dramatic and mesmerizing scene. The nearby Whirlpool Aero Car, a cable car that travels over the rapids, offers visitors a bird's-eye view of the icy whirlpool below. While the Aero Car is usually closed during the winter months, the lookout points along the Niagara Parkway provide excellent views of the frozen rapids.

For those interested in history and culture, winter is a great time to visit some of the region's museums and historic sites. The Niagara Falls History Museum, located just a short distance from the falls, offers fascinating exhibits on the history of the falls, including the geology of the region, the daredevils who attempted to conquer the falls, and the Indigenous peoples who first inhabited the area. Visitors can also learn about the important role that Niagara Falls played in the War of 1812, as well as its significance in the development of hydroelectric power. The museum's indoor exhibits provide a cozy and educational retreat from the winter chill.

Winter is also a quieter time to visit Niagara Falls, as the crowds are smaller and the pace of life slows down. This allows visitors to fully appreciate the natural beauty of the falls without the hustle and bustle of the busy summer months. With fewer tourists, there's more opportunity to take in the serene, peaceful atmosphere of the falls and surrounding parks. The sound of the rushing water is even more pronounced in the stillness of winter, and the snow-covered landscape adds to the sense of calm and isolation.

Accommodations in Niagara Falls are plentiful year-round, and many hotels offer special winter packages that include discounts on rooms, meals, and attractions. Some hotels also feature indoor pools, spas, and other amenities that make for a relaxing winter getaway. Staying in a hotel with a view of the falls is especially rewarding in winter, as guests can wake up to the sight of the frozen falls glistening in the morning light, or watch the nightly illumination from the warmth and comfort of their room.

For those seeking a romantic winter escape, Niagara Falls offers the perfect setting. The icy beauty of the falls, combined with the cozy atmosphere of the nearby hotels and restaurants, makes it an ideal destination for couples. Winter walks along the falls, followed by a warm meal at one of the area's many fine dining establishments, create a memorable and intimate experience. Many hotels offer special romance packages that include champagne, chocolates, and other amenities to enhance the experience.

In conclusion, visiting Niagara Falls in winter is a truly magical experience that offers a unique perspective on this iconic natural wonder. From the frozen cascades and sparkling ice formations to the serene snow-covered parks and thrilling winter activities, the falls take on a completely different character in the colder months. Whether you're seeking adventure, relaxation, or simply the chance to witness the falls in their winter glory, Niagara Falls in winter offers something for everyone. The quiet beauty of the season, combined with the dramatic power of the falls, makes for an unforgettable winter getaway that will leave visitors with lasting memories.

Chapter 13: The Bridges Over Niagara

The bridges over Niagara Falls have a rich history, blending engineering marvels with breathtaking scenery and historical significance. These bridges serve not only as vital transportation links between the United States and Canada but also as iconic structures that offer visitors an unparalleled view of the natural wonder of Niagara Falls and the mighty Niagara River below. Spanning the river at various points near the falls, these bridges provide a connection between the two countries while showcasing the immense power of human ingenuity in overcoming natural barriers. Each bridge over the Niagara River tells a unique story of architectural prowess, historical events, and the deep ties between the two nations. Exploring the history and importance of these bridges reveals their crucial role in shaping the region's identity and facilitating tourism, trade, and cultural exchange.

One of the most famous and recognizable bridges over Niagara is the Rainbow Bridge. Located downstream from the falls, it connects the cities of Niagara Falls, New York, and Niagara Falls, Ontario, offering both vehicles and pedestrians a dramatic view of the Horseshoe Falls, the largest and most powerful of Niagara's three waterfalls. Opened in 1941, the Rainbow Bridge replaced the earlier Honeymoon Bridge, which had collapsed in 1938 due to ice jams and structural failure. The Rainbow Bridge was built with enhanced engineering techniques to withstand the harsh winters and the powerful forces of the river. The bridge quickly became a symbol of resilience and renewal, as well as a popular spot for tourists to take in the magnificent views of the falls and the surrounding area.

The Rainbow Bridge stands as a testament to the cooperation between the United States and Canada. Its construction during a time of international tension, just before the U.S. entered World War II, highlighted the peaceful relationship between the two countries. The bridge was named in honor of this friendship, as well as for the beautiful rainbows that often form in the mist of Niagara Falls. For those who walk across the Rainbow Bridge, the view of the falls is nothing short of spectacular. Visitors can stop in the middle of the bridge, where they are standing on the international boundary line, and gaze at the cascading waters, the swirling mist, and the vibrant rainbows that dance above the river. This experience offers a rare opportunity to appreciate the natural and man-made wonders simultaneously, as the bridge seems to hover over the rushing waters, blending seamlessly with the landscape.

In addition to its scenic and symbolic significance, the Rainbow Bridge plays a vital role in cross-border travel and trade. It is one of the busiest international bridges in North America, with millions of vehicles and pedestrians crossing each year. For visitors, it provides easy access to attractions on both sides of the border, from the Clifton Hill entertainment district in Canada to the Niagara Falls State Park in the U.S. The bridge's location so close to the falls makes it a key link in the region's tourism infrastructure, allowing travelers to explore both countries with ease and enjoy the various viewpoints and activities on each side. Whether it's shopping, dining, or visiting historical landmarks, the Rainbow Bridge serves as a gateway to the rich experiences that Niagara Falls has to offer.

Further downstream, the Whirlpool Rapids Bridge is another significant structure over the Niagara River. This bridge, originally known as the Lower Steel Arch Bridge, was opened in 1897 and is renowned for its unique design. It is a two-level bridge, with one level for vehicular traffic and the other for trains, making it a crucial link for both rail and road transportation between the U.S. and Canada. The Whirlpool Rapids Bridge spans the river at a point where the water roars through the narrow gorge, creating some of the most turbulent rapids in the world. The bridge is named for the famous Whirlpool Rapids below, where the river's powerful currents form swirling vortexes that have captivated visitors for generations.

The Whirlpool Rapids Bridge is an engineering marvel, particularly for its time. It was one of the first bridges to use a steel arch design, which allowed for greater strength and durability. This design was necessary to withstand the immense forces of the river, as well as the heavy loads from both trains and vehicles. Over the years, the bridge has been strengthened and modernized, but its original design remains a testament to the ingenuity and foresight of its builders. Today, the bridge continues to serve as a vital transportation link, particularly for freight trains and passenger vehicles. For visitors, the bridge offers a stunning view of the river and the rapids below, with the cliffs of the Niagara Gorge rising dramatically on either side. Standing on the bridge, one can feel the raw power of the river, as the water churns and crashes through the gorge, creating a sense of awe and wonder.

The Whirlpool Rapids Bridge is also notable for being one of the few bridges in the world that is restricted to Nexus pass holders for vehicle crossings. Nexus is a joint program between the U.S. and Canadian governments that allows pre-approved travelers to cross the border quickly and easily. This makes the bridge a convenient and efficient route for frequent travelers between the two countries, particularly those who live in the Niagara region. The restricted access helps reduce traffic congestion and ensures a smoother crossing experience for those with Nexus passes, while the nearby Rainbow and Lewiston-Queenston bridges handle the bulk of general traffic.

Another important bridge over Niagara is the Lewiston-Queenston Bridge, located further north of the falls. This bridge connects the towns of Lewiston, New York, and Queenston, Ontario, and is primarily used for vehicular traffic. Opened in 1962, the Lewiston-Queenston Bridge is the longest of the Niagara River bridges, spanning a distance of 1,600 feet across the river. It serves as a major route for both commercial and passenger vehicles, particularly for those traveling between Toronto and the eastern United States.

The bridge is a key component of the region's transportation network, facilitating the movement of goods and people across the border.

The Lewiston-Queenston Bridge also holds historical significance, as it is located near the site of the Battle of Queenston Heights, a pivotal battle during the War of 1812 between the United States and British forces. The battle was fought on October 13, 1812, and resulted in a British victory, helping to secure Canada's border against American invasion. Today, visitors to the bridge can explore the nearby Queenston Heights Park, where a monument stands in honor of Major General Sir Isaac Brock, the British commander who was killed during the battle. The park offers sweeping views of the Niagara River and the surrounding landscape, as well as historical plaques and markers that tell the story of the battle and its significance in shaping the history of the region.

The Lewiston-Queenston Bridge is also closely linked to the power generation facilities along the Niagara River. The Sir Adam Beck Hydroelectric Generating Stations, located just upstream from the bridge on the Canadian side, harness the power of the river to produce electricity for millions of people in Ontario and New York. The Robert Moses Niagara Power Plant, located on the U.S. side, also uses the river's energy to generate electricity. The bridge provides a striking view of these massive power plants, which are a testament to the ingenuity and innovation that have made Niagara Falls a leader in hydroelectric power.

While the Rainbow, Whirlpool Rapids, and Lewiston-Queenston bridges are the most famous, they are not the only bridges over the Niagara River. Several smaller bridges, including pedestrian and railway bridges, cross the river at various points along its course. These bridges, though less well-known, play an important role in connecting the communities along the river and providing access to the many parks and recreational areas that line the Niagara Gorge. For example, the pedestrian bridges in the Niagara Glen Nature Reserve allow hikers to explore the trails and rock formations along the gorge, while offering stunning views of the river and the rapids below.

In addition to their practical purposes, the bridges over Niagara also serve as symbols of the close relationship between the United States and Canada. For centuries, the river has been both a natural barrier and a point of connection between the two countries. The bridges that span the river reflect this duality, serving as gateways for trade, tourism, and cultural exchange. The ease with which people can cross from one side to the other underscores the peaceful and cooperative relationship between the two nations, a relationship that has been built on mutual respect and shared interests.

The bridges over Niagara Falls offer much more than just a way to cross the river. They are engineering masterpieces, historical landmarks, and vantage points for some of the most stunning views in the world. From the elegant arches of the Rainbow Bridge to the towering span of the Lewiston-Queenston Bridge, each structure tells a story of innovation, resilience, and collaboration. For visitors, crossing one of these bridges is not just a way to get from one country to another—it's an experience that brings them closer to the natural beauty, history, and spirit of Niagara Falls. Whether by car, train, or on foot, a journey across the Niagara River is an unforgettable part of any visit to this iconic destination.

Chapter 14: Niagara Falls at Night

Niagara Falls at night is a mesmerizing spectacle, transforming one of the world's most famous natural wonders into a magical display of color, light, and sound. As the sun sets and the daytime hustle of tourists slows, a new energy takes over the falls, one that captivates visitors in an entirely different way. The illuminated falls glow in a kaleidoscope of hues, casting a surreal and otherworldly beauty over the thundering waterfalls and the surrounding landscape. For many, seeing Niagara Falls at night is a once-in-a-lifetime experience, offering a unique perspective on this natural wonder and highlighting the harmony between nature and technology. Whether viewed from afar or up close, the sight of the falls lit up in vibrant colors is nothing short of breathtaking.

The most striking feature of Niagara Falls at night is the illumination of the falls themselves. Every evening, a powerful array of colored lights is projected onto the cascading waters, turning the Horseshoe Falls, American Falls, and Bridal Veil Falls into stunning, multi-colored spectacles. These lights are carefully positioned to ensure maximum coverage and brilliance, making the waterfalls seem to glow from within. The colors change throughout the night, cycling through shades of blue, pink, red, green, purple, and gold, creating an ever-changing canvas of light and water. The reflections of these colors shimmer on the surface of the Niagara River, adding to the enchanting atmosphere.

The nightly illumination of Niagara Falls has a long and storied history. It began in 1860, when the falls were first lit in honor of a visit by the Prince of Wales (later King Edward VII). At that time, the lights were rudimentary by today's standards, consisting of a few colored lamps placed on the Canadian side of the river. However, even this modest display was enough to capture the imagination of onlookers and set the stage for what would become a nightly tradition. Over the years, the lighting system has evolved significantly, with modern technology allowing for more powerful, energy-efficient lights and a wider range of colors.

Today, the Niagara Falls Illumination Board oversees the lighting of the falls. The board, which includes representatives from both the United States and Canada, works to ensure that the lighting is both environmentally responsible and visually stunning. In 2016, a major upgrade to the lighting system was completed, replacing the older Xenon lights with LED lights. This new system is not only brighter and more vibrant but also more energy-efficient, using 82 percent less power than the previous system. The LED lights are also capable of producing a wider spectrum of colors, allowing for more intricate and dynamic displays.

The lighting schedule at Niagara Falls varies throughout the year, with the falls illuminated for longer periods during the summer months when the days are longer and the weather is warmer. In the peak summer season, the lights typically come on at dusk and stay on until midnight, while during the winter months, the falls are illuminated for shorter periods due to the earlier sunsets and colder temperatures. Special light shows are often held during holidays or significant events, adding to the festive atmosphere. For example, the falls are bathed in red and white on Canada Day and in red, white, and blue for the Fourth of July, creating a patriotic display that reflects the close ties between the two countries.

One of the best ways to experience Niagara Falls at night is to take a stroll along the illuminated pathways that line the falls on both the American and Canadian sides. These paths offer stunning views of the illuminated waterfalls and the surrounding landscape, with the lights creating a dreamlike ambiance that makes the entire area feel like a living painting. From these vantage points, visitors can see the full expanse of the falls, from the roaring cascade of the Horseshoe Falls to the graceful flow of the American and Bridal Veil Falls. The combination of the illuminated waterfalls and the mist rising from the river creates an ethereal atmosphere that feels almost otherworldly.

For those looking to get even closer to the action, a nighttime boat tour is an unforgettable experience. The Maid of the Mist on the American side and the Hornblower Niagara Cruises on the Canadian side offer evening cruises that take visitors right up to the base of the falls, where they can feel the full force of the water as it crashes down into the river below. These boat tours are especially popular at night, as they provide a front-row seat to the illuminated falls and allow passengers to experience the falls from a perspective that few get to see. The sight of the falls lit up against the night sky, combined with the roar of the water and the cool spray of the mist, creates a sensory experience unlike any other.

In addition to the illumination of the falls, Niagara Falls at night is often accompanied by spectacular fireworks displays. These fireworks are launched from a platform near the falls and light up the night sky with dazzling bursts of color and sound. The fireworks are a highlight of the evening for many visitors, adding an extra layer of excitement and celebration to the nighttime experience. During the summer months, fireworks are typically held on select nights, while special displays are often organized for holidays and major events. The combination of the illuminated falls and the fireworks creates a truly magical atmosphere, as the bursts of light and color reflect off the water and mist, enhancing the already stunning visuals.

Beyond the falls themselves, the surrounding area also comes alive at night. Both the American and Canadian sides of the falls offer a range of activities and attractions that are best experienced after dark. On the Canadian side, Clifton Hill is a popular destination for families and visitors of all ages. Known as the "Street of Fun," Clifton Hill is home to a variety of entertainment options, including arcades, amusement rides, restaurants, and shops. The street is brightly lit with neon lights, adding to the festive atmosphere and making it a fun place to explore after a visit to the falls. Visitors can enjoy a ride on the Niagara SkyWheel, a giant Ferris wheel that offers panoramic views of the falls and the surrounding area, or take in the vibrant nightlife at one of the many bars and clubs in the area.

On the American side, the Niagara Falls State Park also offers nighttime activities, including guided tours and illuminated walkways that provide a closer view of the falls. The park's scenic overlooks and observation decks are open to visitors, allowing them to take in the illuminated falls from different angles. For those interested in learning more about the history and geology of the falls, the park's Visitor Center offers exhibits and displays that delve into the fascinating story of Niagara Falls. The park is also home to the Niagara Falls Observation Tower, which extends out over the gorge and provides one of the best vantage points for viewing the falls at night.

Niagara Falls at night is not just about the visual spectacle, but also the sounds of the falls, which seem to take on a new dimension after dark. As the day winds down and the crowds begin to thin, the roar of the waterfalls becomes more pronounced, filling the air with a deep, resonant hum that reverberates throughout the area. The sound of the water crashing against the rocks below is both powerful and soothing, creating a sense of awe and wonder that is heightened by the stillness of the night. For many visitors, simply standing in the presence of the falls at night, listening to the water and watching the ever-changing colors of the illumination, is a deeply moving and unforgettable experience.

In the winter, Niagara Falls at night takes on a different kind of beauty. As the temperatures drop, the mist from the falls freezes, creating a landscape of ice and snow that looks like something out of a fairy tale. The illuminated falls are framed by icicles and frozen formations, while the surrounding trees and pathways are often covered in a shimmering layer of frost. The winter illumination of the falls is particularly striking, as the colors of the lights reflect off the ice and snow, creating a dazzling display of light and texture. Winter visitors can enjoy the beauty of the falls from one of the many heated viewing areas or take a leisurely walk along the illuminated pathways, where the crisp winter air adds to the sense of magic and wonder.

Niagara Falls at night is truly a sight to behold. Whether viewed from the vantage points along the river, aboard a boat at the base of the falls, or from one of the surrounding attractions, the illuminated waterfalls offer a unique and unforgettable experience. The combination of the natural beauty of the falls, the vibrant colors of the lights, and the festive atmosphere of the surrounding area creates a one-of-a-kind destination that continues to captivate visitors from around the world. Whether it's a romantic evening for two, a family outing, or a solo adventure, Niagara Falls at night is an experience that leaves a lasting impression on all who visit.

Chapter 15: The Famous Maid of the Mist

The *Maid of the Mist* is one of the most iconic and enduring symbols of Niagara Falls, offering visitors an unparalleled experience of the mighty waterfall for over a century. This famous boat tour provides a thrilling, close-up view of the falls, immersing passengers in the power, mist, and roar of one of the most magnificent natural wonders of the world. A journey on the *Maid of the Mist* is not just a boat ride; it is a rite of passage for many who visit Niagara Falls, an experience that brings you face-to-face with the grandeur and force of nature in a way that few other activities can match.

The history of the *Maid of the Mist* dates back to 1846, when the first version of the boat service was launched. Originally, it wasn't meant to be a sightseeing tour but rather a mode of transportation across the Niagara River, helping to connect the United States and Canada. At the time, the boat was powered by steam and carried passengers, cargo, and even horses and carriages across the river. However, in 1848, the opening of a suspension bridge over the river made this service obsolete. Rather than shutting down, the owners of the *Maid of the Mist* decided to repurpose the boat for sightseeing, taking advantage of its unique proximity to the world-famous waterfalls.

This decision proved to be a brilliant one, as Niagara Falls was already becoming a popular destination for travelers and tourists from around the world. In the mid-19th century, with improvements in transportation and infrastructure, Niagara Falls became more accessible, attracting a growing number of visitors eager to witness its beauty and power. The newly repurposed *Maid of the Mist* began offering tours that brought passengers right up to the base of the falls, allowing them to experience the awe-inspiring force of the cascading water firsthand.

Over the years, the *Maid of the Mist* has evolved alongside the increasing number of visitors and advancements in technology. The original steam-powered boat was replaced by more modern vessels as the demand for tours grew. In 1885, Niagara Falls became one of the first state parks in the United States, and tourism to the area increased even further. As a result, the *Maid of the Mist* became an essential part of the Niagara Falls experience, solidifying its reputation as a must-do activity for visitors.

One of the most thrilling aspects of the *Maid of the Mist* experience is the boat's route, which takes passengers as close as possible to the falls. The tour begins at a dock on the U.S. side of the river, where passengers board the boat and are outfitted with rain ponchos—an essential item for this adventure, as the mist from the falls is so thick that you are guaranteed to get wet. As the boat sets off, it makes its way along the Niagara River, passing the American Falls and Bridal Veil Falls before heading straight into the heart of Horseshoe Falls, the largest and most powerful of the three waterfalls that make up Niagara Falls.

As the *Maid of the Mist* approaches Horseshoe Falls, the experience becomes even more exhilarating. The boat is surrounded by the deafening roar of the water as it crashes down into the river below, and the mist rises up in great plumes, drenching the passengers. The power and magnitude of the falls are on full display as the boat inches closer to the base of the cascade, offering a view that few people ever get to see up close. The experience of standing on the deck of the *Maid of the Mist*, feeling the spray of the water and hearing the thunderous sound of the falls, is nothing short of awe-inspiring. It's an encounter with nature at its most powerful, a moment that leaves a lasting impression on all who experience it.

Throughout its long history, the *Maid of the Mist* has become more than just a boat tour—it has become a cultural icon and a symbol of Niagara Falls itself. The name "Maid of the Mist" is derived from an ancient Iroquois legend about a young woman who, after losing her husband, entered the Niagara River in a canoe, hoping to find peace in the afterlife by going over the falls. According to the legend, she was saved by the thunder god, Hinum, who lived beneath the falls, and was transformed into a spirit that protected the waters. This mythical story has added to the mystique and allure of the boat tour, connecting it to the rich cultural history of the region.

Over the years, millions of people have taken the *Maid of the Mist* tour, including famous dignitaries, celebrities, and even royalty. Among the most notable passengers was President Abraham Lincoln, who took the tour in 1857 before his presidency, and Princess Diana, who visited Niagara Falls with her sons in 1991. The *Maid of the Mist* has also been featured in numerous films, television shows, and documentaries, further cementing its status as a symbol of Niagara Falls.

Despite the passage of time and the changes in technology, the essence of the *Maid of the Mist* experience has remained the same—offering visitors a front-row seat to one of the most extraordinary natural wonders on Earth. Today, the boats used for the tour are powered by electric motors, making them more environmentally friendly and quieter than their predecessors. The switch to electric boats, which took place in 2020, was a significant milestone in the history of the *Maid of the Mist*, reflecting the growing awareness of environmental sustainability and the importance of protecting the natural beauty of Niagara Falls for future generations.

The modern *Maid of the Mist* boats are equipped with state-of-the-art technology, ensuring that passengers have a safe and comfortable journey while still providing an up-close and personal experience with the falls. The boats are designed to navigate the powerful currents of the Niagara River and withstand the intense conditions created by the mist and the force of the falling water. Despite the challenges posed by the river's strong currents and the sheer power of the falls, the *Maid of the Mist* has maintained an impeccable safety record, allowing visitors of all ages to enjoy the experience without worry.

The tour typically lasts about 20 minutes, but the memories created during that short time often last a lifetime. Many visitors describe the experience as humbling, as it provides a new perspective on the sheer force and scale of Niagara Falls. Standing on the deck of the *Maid of the Mist*, surrounded by the swirling mist and the sound of the rushing water, passengers are reminded of the incredible power of nature and the wonders of the natural world. It is a sensory experience like no other, one that leaves you feeling connected to the forces of the Earth in a profound way.

In addition to offering an unforgettable experience for tourists, the *Maid of the Mist* has also played a role in scientific and environmental research. Over the years, researchers and scientists have used the boat to study the geological formations around the falls, as well as the effects of erosion and water flow on the surrounding landscape. This research has helped to deepen our understanding of the falls and ensure that they are preserved for future generations.

The *Maid of the Mist* is more than just a boat ride—it's an integral part of the Niagara Falls experience, offering a unique and exhilarating way to connect with one of the most awe-inspiring natural wonders in the world. For many visitors, it's the highlight of their trip, a moment of wonder and excitement that they will never forget. Whether it's your first time visiting Niagara Falls or you're a seasoned traveler returning for another adventure, a journey on the *Maid of the Mist* is an absolute must. It's an experience that brings you face-to-face with the raw power of nature, leaving you in awe of the beauty and majesty of Niagara Falls.

Chapter 16: The American and Bridal Veil Falls

The American and Bridal Veil Falls are two of the three waterfalls that together make up the iconic Niagara Falls, the third being the Horseshoe Falls. While Horseshoe Falls often captures the most attention due to its sheer size and volume, the American and Bridal Veil Falls possess their own distinct beauty and charm. These waterfalls are located on the U.S. side of the Niagara River and, despite being smaller than their Canadian counterpart, they are no less significant in their contribution to the stunning natural landscape of Niagara Falls. Together, the American and Bridal Veil Falls offer visitors breathtaking views, fascinating geological formations, and an opportunity to experience the power of nature up close.

The American Falls, the second-largest of the three waterfalls, spans roughly 830 feet (253 meters) across and drops about 90 to 110 feet (27 to 34 meters) into the rocky basin below. What sets the American Falls apart from Horseshoe Falls is the manner in which the water tumbles down over large boulders, creating a spectacular cascade of water that looks as if it is crashing over steps made of stone. The combination of water flowing over these rocks creates an ever-changing pattern of flow, which makes each view of the falls slightly different depending on the time of day and the water level in the river. The powerful rush of water, combined with the natural rock formations at the base, creates a scene of rugged beauty that captivates all who visit.

One of the defining features of the American Falls is the accumulation of talus—large rocks that have broken away from the cliff due to the process of erosion and have collected at the base of the waterfall. Over time, the powerful force of the water has worn away the underlying rock, causing periodic rockslides that contribute to the talus pile. This natural process of erosion has reshaped the American Falls over thousands of years, giving it its unique structure and appearance. The rocks at the bottom of the falls range in size, some of them quite massive, and they cause the water to splash and crash in an irregular, dramatic fashion as it plunges to the river below. This rugged landscape makes the American Falls stand out in contrast to the more graceful, smooth curves of Horseshoe Falls.

Directly adjacent to the American Falls is the smaller yet equally captivating Bridal Veil Falls. This waterfall is named for its delicate, veil-like appearance, as the water cascades gently down the rocks in a thin, flowing sheet that resembles a bridal veil. Bridal Veil Falls is the smallest of the three Niagara Falls, measuring about 56 feet (17 meters) wide and dropping around 78 feet (24 meters) into the Niagara Gorge. Despite its smaller size, Bridal Veil Falls possesses a quiet elegance that adds to the overall beauty of the Niagara Falls experience.

Bridal Veil Falls is separated from the American Falls by Luna Island, a small piece of land that divides the two waterfalls. Visitors to Luna Island can stand between the American and Bridal Veil Falls, taking in the magnificent views from this unique vantage point. The proximity of the two waterfalls allows for a more intimate experience with the falls, as the island is positioned right at the edge of the rushing water, giving visitors a sense of being surrounded by the force and beauty of Niagara Falls. From this location, the thundering sound of the falls, combined with the mist that rises from the plunging water, creates a sensory experience that leaves a lasting impression.

One of the most memorable aspects of visiting Bridal Veil Falls is the opportunity to take the Cave of the Winds tour, which brings visitors to the base of the waterfall, providing an up-close and immersive experience with the power of the falls. The tour begins with an elevator ride down into the Niagara Gorge, followed by a series of wooden walkways that lead right up to the base of Bridal Veil Falls. Known as the "Hurricane Deck," the final platform allows visitors to stand just a few feet away from the rushing water, where they can feel the full force of the mist and the wind created by the waterfall. The sensation of standing so close to the falls, with water pouring down all around you and the roar of the falls filling the air, is unforgettable. It's an opportunity to experience the raw power of nature in a way that few other attractions can offer.

The American and Bridal Veil Falls, while smaller than Horseshoe Falls, are essential parts of the Niagara Falls ecosystem and have played significant roles in the history and geology of the region. The water that flows over these falls comes from the upper Great Lakes, particularly Lake Erie, and flows through the Niagara River before making its dramatic descent over the falls and continuing its journey to Lake Ontario. This continuous flow of water has carved out the Niagara Gorge over millennia, shaping the landscape that visitors see today.

The history of the American and Bridal Veil Falls is closely tied to the development of Niagara Falls as a popular tourist destination. In the 19th century, as more people began to visit the falls, the area around the American and Bridal Veil Falls became a hub of activity, with hotels, parks, and viewing platforms constructed to accommodate the growing number of tourists. One of the earliest and most famous viewing platforms was Terrapin Point, a small rock outcropping that allowed visitors to stand directly over the edge of the American Falls. Although erosion has since reshaped this area, the desire to get as close to the falls as possible has been a consistent theme in the history of Niagara Falls tourism.

In addition to their role in tourism, the American and Bridal Veil Falls have also been the focus of scientific study, particularly in relation to erosion and the natural forces that continue to shape the falls. In the mid-20th century, concerns about the rate of erosion at the American Falls led to a major project to stabilize the area. In 1969, the American Falls were temporarily "shut off" by diverting the flow of the Niagara River in order to study the effects of erosion and to assess the stability of the rock face. This extraordinary event allowed scientists and engineers to walk along the dry riverbed and make important observations about the geological processes at work. The project ultimately resulted in efforts to slow the rate of erosion and preserve the falls for future generations.

The American and Bridal Veil Falls are not only a testament to the power of water but also a reminder of the delicate balance between nature and human intervention. Over the years, efforts have been made to protect and preserve the natural beauty of the falls while allowing millions of people to experience their majesty. The creation of the Niagara Falls State Park, the oldest state park in the United States, has ensured that the land around the falls remains a protected area, allowing visitors to enjoy the falls in a natural and scenic setting.

While the American and Bridal Veil Falls are spectacular to see during the day, they take on an entirely different appearance at night. After the sun sets, both waterfalls are illuminated with vibrant, colorful lights that transform the cascading water into a mesmerizing display. The Niagara Falls Illumination, which lights up all three waterfalls, including the American and Bridal Veil Falls, is a nightly tradition that has been enchanting visitors for decades. The sight of the falls glowing in shades of blue, purple, red, and green is breathtaking, offering a magical and otherworldly view of this natural wonder.

In winter, the American and Bridal Veil Falls offer yet another unique perspective, as the freezing temperatures cause the mist from the falls to form ice sculptures and snow-covered landscapes. The area around the falls becomes a winter wonderland, with ice forming along the riverbanks and on the rocks at the base of the falls. Although the water continues to flow, the icy formations create a surreal and enchanting scene that showcases the beauty of Niagara Falls in every season.

In conclusion, the American and Bridal Veil Falls are integral parts of the Niagara Falls experience. They offer a unique and rugged beauty that complements the more well-known Horseshoe Falls, providing visitors with a different perspective on the power and majesty of Niagara Falls. From the dramatic cascades of the American Falls to the delicate beauty of Bridal Veil Falls, these waterfalls invite visitors to connect with nature and experience the wonder of one of the world's most famous natural landmarks. Whether you're standing at the edge of the falls on Luna Island, exploring the base of Bridal Veil Falls on the Cave of the Winds tour, or admiring the illuminated waterfalls at night, the American and Bridal Veil Falls offer an unforgettable journey into the heart of Niagara Falls.

Chapter 17: The Horseshoe Falls Experience

The Horseshoe Falls, the most iconic and largest of the three waterfalls that make up Niagara Falls, is a natural marvel that has captivated the hearts and minds of visitors for centuries. Named for its distinctive horseshoe-shaped curve, this awe-inspiring waterfall straddles the border between Canada and the United States, with most of it located on the Canadian side. The Horseshoe Falls is renowned not only for its immense size and power but also for the immersive experience it offers to those who come to witness its breathtaking beauty. Standing before this mighty waterfall is an encounter with nature's raw power, as millions of gallons of water thunder over the edge every minute, creating a spectacle that is both humbling and exhilarating.

At approximately 2,600 feet (790 meters) wide and 167 feet (51 meters) tall, the Horseshoe Falls is the largest and most powerful waterfall in North America. On average, over 90% of the water that flows over Niagara Falls goes over the Horseshoe Falls, making it a massive force of nature. The Niagara River, which serves as the source of the falls, drains water from the Great Lakes, the largest group of freshwater lakes in the world. As this water approaches the edge of the Horseshoe Falls, it gathers speed, and the sound of the rushing river grows louder and louder until it reaches a deafening crescendo as it plunges into the gorge below. The sheer volume of water, combined with the height of the drop, creates a constant roar that reverberates throughout the area, leaving visitors in awe of the power of nature.

One of the most remarkable aspects of the Horseshoe Falls experience is the ever-present mist that rises from the bottom of the falls. As the water crashes into the rocks and pool below, it sends up a massive cloud of mist that can be seen from miles away. This mist often creates rainbows on sunny days, adding to the magic of the experience.

Visitors who get close to the falls—whether from viewing platforms, boats, or other attractions—are often greeted by the cool spray of the mist, which can leave them drenched, especially on windy days. The mist gives the Horseshoe Falls an ethereal, otherworldly quality, as if the entire landscape is shrouded in a perpetual fog. For many, the sensation of being enveloped by the mist is one of the highlights of visiting the falls, offering a tangible reminder of the immense power at work.

There are several ways to experience the majesty of the Horseshoe Falls, each offering a unique perspective on this natural wonder. Perhaps the most iconic and well-known way to get up close and personal with the Horseshoe Falls is by taking a ride on the Maid of the Mist, a boat tour that has been operating since the 19th century. The Maid of the Mist offers passengers a front-row seat to the power and beauty of the falls, as the boat ventures into the basin at the base of Horseshoe Falls. As the boat approaches the falls, the roar of the water becomes almost deafening, and passengers are surrounded by the thick mist that rises from the crashing water. The experience is thrilling, as the boat seems to disappear into the mist, leaving visitors with an unforgettable view of the falls from below. The Maid of the Mist provides a visceral, up-close encounter with Horseshoe Falls that leaves a lasting impression on all who take the ride.

Another way to experience the Horseshoe Falls is by visiting Table Rock, a popular observation area located right at the edge of the falls on the Canadian side. From here, visitors can stand just feet away from the rushing water as it plunges over the edge. The proximity to the falls from this vantage point is awe-inspiring, as visitors can feel the ground tremble beneath them and hear the thunderous roar of the water as it cascades down. The sheer volume of water flowing over the edge—an average of about 168,000 cubic meters per minute during peak flow—creates a powerful and mesmerizing sight. Onlookers are often struck by the immense force of the water, which seems almost unstoppable as it surges over the precipice and into the gorge below.

For those seeking an even closer view of the Horseshoe Falls, the Journey Behind the Falls offers an incredible opportunity to experience the falls from a completely different perspective. This unique attraction takes visitors through a series of tunnels carved into the rock behind the waterfall, leading to two observation decks located directly behind the curtain of water. Standing behind the falls, visitors can feel the ground shake as the water crashes down just a few feet in front of them. The sound of the water is overwhelming, and the mist is thick, creating an immersive and unforgettable experience. From these vantage points, visitors can see the falls from a rarely seen angle, gaining a deeper appreciation for the power and beauty of Horseshoe Falls.

The Horseshoe Falls is not only a natural wonder but also a source of inspiration and fascination for people from all walks of life. Over the centuries, it has drawn explorers, adventurers, artists, and daredevils who have been captivated by its power and beauty. The falls have been the subject of countless paintings, photographs, and literary works, each attempting to capture the essence of this majestic landscape. For indigenous peoples, the falls have long held spiritual significance, representing a sacred site where the forces of nature are at their most powerful. Even today, the falls continue to inspire a sense of wonder and awe in those who visit, reminding us of the beauty and strength of the natural world.

The Horseshoe Falls experience is not limited to daytime viewing. At night, the falls are illuminated with vibrant, colorful lights, creating a magical and surreal scene that is truly unforgettable. The Niagara Falls Illumination has been a beloved tradition for decades, and seeing the Horseshoe Falls bathed in shades of blue, purple, red, and green is a highlight for many visitors. The lights highlight the curves of the falls and the mist, transforming the landscape into a glowing, dreamlike spectacle. The combination of the illuminated water, the mist, and the surrounding darkness creates a mesmerizing display that captivates visitors and offers a completely different experience from seeing the falls during the day.

In addition to its natural beauty, the Horseshoe Falls is also a symbol of human ingenuity and progress. The immense power of the falls has been harnessed for hydroelectric power generation, providing electricity to millions of people in both Canada and the United States. The development of hydroelectric power at Niagara Falls in the late 19th and early 20th centuries marked a significant achievement in the history of energy production, and it continues to play a crucial role in powering the surrounding region today. The ability to harness the power of the falls while preserving their natural beauty is a testament to the balance between nature and technology, and it highlights the importance of sustainable energy practices.

The Horseshoe Falls experience is also enhanced by the surrounding natural beauty of the Niagara region. The Niagara River, which flows into the falls, is a picturesque waterway surrounded by lush greenery and scenic vistas. The Niagara Gorge, carved out by the force of the water over thousands of years, offers stunning views and hiking opportunities for those looking to explore the area further. Niagara Falls State Park, the oldest state park in the United States, provides ample space for visitors to enjoy the natural landscape, with walking paths, picnic areas, and scenic overlooks that offer panoramic views of the falls and the river. The beauty of the region, combined with the majesty of the falls, creates a perfect environment for visitors to connect with nature and enjoy outdoor activities.

Winter at Horseshoe Falls offers yet another unique experience. As the temperatures drop, the mist from the falls freezes, creating stunning ice formations along the riverbanks and on the rocks at the base of the falls. The area is transformed into a winter wonderland, with snow and ice covering the landscape, adding a new layer of beauty to the already breathtaking scenery. While the water continues to flow, the frozen mist creates the illusion of a frozen waterfall, making for an incredible sight. Visitors brave enough to visit in the winter are rewarded with a quieter, more peaceful experience, as the falls are less crowded during the colder months.

In conclusion, the Horseshoe Falls experience is one that leaves a lasting impact on all who visit. Whether you're standing at the edge of the falls at Table Rock, feeling the mist on a Maid of the Mist boat tour, or venturing behind the waterfall on the Journey Behind the Falls, the power and beauty of Horseshoe Falls are undeniable. This iconic waterfall, with its immense size, thunderous roar, and ever-present mist, offers a sensory experience that is unlike anything else in the world. It is a place where visitors can connect with the forces of nature, marvel at the power of water, and be inspired by the beauty of the natural world. The Horseshoe Falls is not just a waterfall—it is a symbol of the majesty and strength of nature, and experiencing it firsthand is an unforgettable journey into the heart of one of the world's most famous natural wonders.

Chapter 18: The Role of Niagara Falls in Movies

Niagara Falls, with its breathtaking beauty, immense power, and awe-inspiring majesty, has long captivated the imagination of filmmakers and moviegoers alike. Its dramatic presence, iconic mist, and thunderous roar make it a perfect cinematic backdrop, lending a sense of grandeur, romance, adventure, and danger to a variety of films. The falls have not only been used as a stunning visual element but have also played integral roles in shaping the narratives of numerous movies. From classic Hollywood films to more contemporary productions, Niagara Falls has become a legendary setting, weaving its natural splendor into the history of cinema.

One of the most iconic films to feature Niagara Falls is the 1953 thriller *Niagara*, starring Marilyn Monroe, Joseph Cotten, and Jean Peters. Directed by Henry Hathaway, this noir film elevated Niagara Falls to a central role, intertwining the majestic landscape with a suspenseful plot about betrayal, passion, and murder. The falls serve as more than just a backdrop in *Niagara*—they are a symbol of the emotional turbulence between the characters. Monroe's character, Rose Loomis, is involved in a dark scheme to kill her husband, and the roaring waters of the falls mirror the tension and intensity of the plot. In several key scenes, the falls loom large, providing a dramatic contrast between the natural beauty of the setting and the sinister motivations of the characters. Monroe's sultry performance is set against the awe-inspiring force of the waterfalls, creating a visually stunning juxtaposition. *Niagara* is one of the earliest films to use the falls in such an immersive way, establishing them not only as a tourist destination but also as a powerful cinematic tool that contributes to the atmosphere of mystery and suspense.

Another film where Niagara Falls takes center stage is the romantic drama *Superman II* (1980). In this sequel to the 1978 superhero film, Superman (played by Christopher Reeve) takes Lois Lane (Margot Kidder) on a romantic trip to Niagara Falls. The falls provide a scenic, picturesque backdrop for their evolving relationship, but the tranquility of the moment is quickly shattered by danger when a young boy falls over the railing and plummets towards the falls. Superman saves the child in a dramatic rescue, showcasing not only his superhuman abilities but also using Niagara Falls as a symbol of both beauty and peril. This moment emphasizes the constant tension between peaceful serenity and the looming possibility of disaster that the falls naturally evoke. The grandeur of Niagara Falls adds an unforgettable layer to the storyline, contributing to the visual impact and emotional depth of the film.

In the world of animation, Niagara Falls has also made memorable appearances. One notable example is in *Looney Tunes* cartoons, where the falls often appear as part of exaggerated slapstick sequences involving characters like Bugs Bunny or Daffy Duck. The falls serve as a dramatic obstacle, with characters frequently finding themselves hurtling towards the edge of the powerful waterfall in comical and over-the-top scenarios. These animated depictions play with the inherent danger of Niagara Falls, turning its fearsome power into an opportunity for humor. While exaggerated, these cartoons capture the public fascination with the falls as a place of adventure and peril, showing how deeply ingrained the falls have become in popular culture.

In more modern films, Niagara Falls continues to be a favored location for its visual impact and symbolic resonance. In *Bruce Almighty* (2003), a comedy starring Jim Carrey, the falls are featured prominently in a humorous news segment where Carrey's character, Bruce Nolan, is reporting live from the falls. In one memorable scene, Bruce's outlandish behavior while reporting from the base of the falls is both comical and visually striking, with the falls roaring behind him as he conducts his chaotic report. The juxtaposition of Niagara Falls' natural grandeur with Bruce's exaggerated antics emphasizes the absurdity of the moment, using the falls as both a literal and figurative force of nature that contrasts with the character's trivial concerns. This scene not only provides comedic value but also reinforces the idea that Niagara Falls is a place where the extraordinary happens, whether in nature or in human behavior.

Niagara Falls has also been the setting for a variety of documentaries and travel films, highlighting the historical, geological, and environmental significance of the falls. Documentaries such as *Niagara: Miracles, Myths, and Magic* (1986) take a deep dive into the history and folklore surrounding the falls, blending factual information with the mystique that has surrounded Niagara for centuries. Through these films, viewers are able to appreciate the natural wonder of Niagara Falls from a variety of perspectives—geological, historical, and cultural. These documentaries not only explore the formation of the falls and their impact on the environment but also delve into the human fascination with the falls over the centuries, including the countless adventurers, daredevils, and tourists who have been drawn to its waters.

In films where Niagara Falls does not play a central role, it often appears in travel montages or as a symbolic element representing the power and beauty of nature. The falls have been used as a setting for emotional reunions, farewells, and moments of personal reflection. In *Pirates of the Caribbean: At World's End* (2007), a fictionalized version of Niagara Falls serves as the gateway to Davy Jones' Locker, highlighting the falls' metaphorical association with the boundary between life and death. In this context, the falls are transformed into an otherworldly, mythical location, demonstrating how filmmakers have continued to tap into the symbolic potential of Niagara Falls, not just as a location, but as a representation of natural forces beyond human control.

Niagara Falls has also been featured in romantic comedies, where it serves as a backdrop for love stories and comedic moments. One such example is the film *The Long Kiss Goodnight* (1996), starring Geena Davis and Samuel L. Jackson. While not primarily focused on the falls, the film's climactic showdown occurs on the Rainbow Bridge, a border crossing near Niagara Falls. The falls loom in the background, providing a striking setting for the intense action scenes. The contrast between the peaceful majesty of the falls and the high-octane drama of the film's final act adds to the tension and visual appeal of the climax, showing how the falls can be used to heighten both romance and danger.

Beyond feature films, Niagara Falls has also appeared in countless television shows, travel series, and commercials, reinforcing its status as an international symbol of natural beauty and power. Its appearance in advertisements, often promoting tourism, has helped maintain its global reputation as a must-see destination. In many ways, the falls are instantly recognizable to viewers, symbolizing grandeur, nature's might, and a sense of timeless wonder. The falls' repeated use in media reflects both their universal appeal and their ability to evoke a wide range of emotions—from awe to fear, from romance to suspense.

Another key aspect of Niagara Falls' role in movies is how it has been used to explore human ambition and the relationship between humanity and nature. The daredevils who have attempted to conquer the falls, whether through tightrope walking or barrel plunges, have inspired films that highlight the falls' inherent danger and allure. These films often center on the idea of testing human limits against nature's most powerful forces. The falls serve as a metaphor for the risks people take in pursuit of glory, freedom, or fame, illustrating the timeless struggle between human determination and the overwhelming power of nature.

The symbolic significance of Niagara Falls extends beyond its sheer physical presence. In many films, it represents the boundary between the known and the unknown, between safety and danger, and even between life and death. The immense power of the water, the seemingly unstoppable force of the current, and the constant threat of being pulled over the edge make the falls an ideal symbol for moments of great personal or narrative transformation. Characters in films who visit Niagara Falls are often on the brink of a major life change, and the falls serve as a visual and thematic marker of this transition.

In conclusion, Niagara Falls' role in movies is vast and varied, ranging from a powerful natural force that shapes the plot of thrillers to a romantic backdrop for love stories. Whether in classic black-and-white films, colorful animated features, or modern blockbusters, the falls have played a vital role in bringing stories to life on the big screen. Their universal appeal and timeless beauty ensure that Niagara Falls will continue to inspire filmmakers and enchant audiences for generations to come. From symbolizing the unpredictability of life to representing the majesty of nature, Niagara Falls remains one of cinema's most enduring and iconic natural settings.

Chapter 19: Protecting Niagara's Natural Beauty

Protecting Niagara's natural beauty is a monumental task that spans generations, bringing together conservationists, government bodies, indigenous communities, and everyday citizens in a shared mission to preserve one of the most iconic natural landmarks in the world. Niagara Falls, with its breathtaking waterfalls, surrounding parks, rivers, wildlife, and ecosystems, is not only a global tourist destination but also an ecological treasure. Its significance goes beyond tourism, as it serves as a critical habitat for various species, a powerful source of renewable energy, and a natural wonder that inspires awe and reverence. The efforts to protect Niagara's beauty reflect a deep respect for the environment, ensuring that this majestic site remains pristine for future generations while balancing human activity with ecological preservation.

Niagara Falls is part of a larger system that includes the Niagara River, the Great Lakes, and the surrounding landscapes. The river itself serves as a border between the United States and Canada, making international cooperation crucial in preserving the falls. The water that plunges over the falls comes from four of the five Great Lakes, which contain nearly 20% of the world's freshwater supply. As such, any environmental degradation in this area could have far-reaching consequences, affecting not only the local ecosystem but also the millions of people who rely on the Great Lakes for drinking water, industry, and agriculture. Protecting the natural beauty of Niagara Falls involves addressing issues such as water quality, pollution, invasive species, habitat destruction, and the pressures of tourism and urban development.

One of the most critical aspects of protecting Niagara's natural beauty is water conservation and management. The sheer volume of water that flows through Niagara Falls each day—over 3,160 tons per second—is staggering. This immense flow of water is essential to the falls' power and visual spectacle, but it also poses challenges for conservationists. The diversion of water for hydroelectric power generation, a practice that began in the late 19th century, has significantly altered the flow of the Niagara River. While hydroelectricity has brought significant economic and environmental benefits, providing renewable energy to millions of people, it also reduces the volume of water cascading over the falls, particularly during non-peak tourist hours when water is diverted to power stations.

The challenge has been to strike a balance between harnessing the power of the river for energy production and maintaining the visual and ecological integrity of the falls. Since the 1950s, agreements between the United States and Canada have regulated the amount of water that can be diverted for hydroelectric power, ensuring that enough water flows over the falls during daylight hours to preserve its grandeur for visitors. At night, when fewer tourists are present, more water is diverted for power generation. This balance is essential to both protecting the falls' natural beauty and ensuring that it remains a sustainable source of clean energy. However, conservationists remain vigilant, ensuring that the flow of water does not dip to levels that would harm the surrounding ecosystems or diminish the falls' iconic appearance.

Pollution control is another vital element in protecting Niagara's natural beauty. Industrialization, urbanization, and agricultural runoff pose threats to the water quality of the Niagara River and the Great Lakes. In the early to mid-20th century, pollution from factories and waste disposal facilities along the river and its tributaries led to significant environmental degradation. Toxic chemicals, heavy metals, and other pollutants entered the water system, causing harm to aquatic life and degrading the quality of the water flowing over Niagara Falls. One of the most infamous environmental disasters in the region was the Love Canal crisis of the 1970s, where hazardous waste buried near Niagara Falls caused widespread contamination, leading to health problems for local residents and prompting a national outcry for stricter environmental regulations.

In response to these issues, both the U.S. and Canadian governments implemented stricter environmental laws aimed at reducing pollution and improving water quality in the Niagara River and the Great Lakes. The Clean Water Act in the U.S. and similar legislation in Canada, along with binational agreements such as the Great Lakes Water Quality Agreement, have helped reduce industrial pollution and improve wastewater treatment. Today, efforts continue to ensure that water flowing over Niagara Falls is clean and that pollutants from industry, agriculture, and urban development are kept in check. Ongoing monitoring and cleanup initiatives are essential to preserving the ecological health of the river and maintaining the natural beauty of the falls.

The introduction and spread of invasive species in the Niagara River and the Great Lakes basin pose another threat to Niagara's natural beauty. Species such as zebra mussels, round gobies, and sea lampreys have disrupted local ecosystems, outcompeting native species for resources and damaging aquatic habitats. Invasive species can alter the balance of ecosystems, reduce biodiversity, and degrade water quality, threatening the health of both aquatic and terrestrial environments around Niagara Falls. Efforts to control invasive species include habitat restoration, public education, and partnerships between governmental agencies, conservation groups, and local communities.

In addition to protecting the water and wildlife, preserving the natural beauty of Niagara Falls involves careful management of the surrounding parks and green spaces. Niagara Falls is bordered by vast parks on both the U.S. and Canadian sides, which are home to a variety of plant and animal species. These parks not only provide a scenic backdrop to the falls but also serve as important habitats for wildlife, from birds and mammals to amphibians and fish. The Niagara Falls State Park in New York, established in 1885, is the oldest state park in the United States, and it plays a crucial role in protecting the natural landscape around the falls. On the Canadian side, the Niagara Parks Commission oversees the management of 56 kilometers (35 miles) of parkland along the Niagara River, ensuring that the natural beauty of the area is preserved while accommodating the millions of tourists who visit each year.

Sustainable tourism is a key consideration in protecting Niagara's natural beauty. With millions of visitors flocking to the falls annually, the impact of human activity on the environment is significant. Erosion, litter, and the construction of infrastructure to accommodate tourists can all contribute to the degradation of natural habitats. Conservationists and park authorities work to minimize these impacts by implementing measures such as eco-friendly transportation options, waste reduction programs, and public education campaigns encouraging visitors to respect the environment. Trails, observation decks, and other tourist facilities are carefully designed to blend with the natural landscape, ensuring that visitors can enjoy the falls without compromising their ecological integrity.

One example of sustainable tourism at Niagara Falls is the use of electric and hybrid-powered tour boats, such as the iconic *Maid of the Mist* and *Hornblower*, which take visitors on close-up excursions to the base of the falls. These boats have been retrofitted to reduce emissions and minimize their environmental footprint, allowing tourists to experience the awe-inspiring power of the falls in a way that is less harmful to the environment. Additionally, many of the facilities in the area, including restaurants and hotels, have adopted green practices such as energy-efficient lighting, recycling programs, and water conservation initiatives.

Education and public awareness are crucial in the efforts to protect Niagara's natural beauty. Conservation organizations and park authorities offer a range of educational programs and initiatives designed to raise awareness about environmental issues and encourage responsible behavior among visitors. Interpretive centers, guided tours, and informational signage throughout the parks provide visitors with insights into the ecological significance of the falls and the surrounding landscapes. These educational efforts foster a sense of stewardship and responsibility, encouraging people to take an active role in protecting the natural beauty of Niagara Falls.

Indigenous communities have also played a vital role in preserving the natural beauty of Niagara Falls. The area around the falls holds deep cultural and spiritual significance for the Haudenosaunee (Iroquois) people, particularly the Seneca Nation, who have lived in the region for centuries. Indigenous knowledge and traditions have long emphasized the importance of living in harmony with nature and protecting the land for future generations. Today, indigenous leaders and organizations continue to be involved in conservation efforts, advocating for the protection of sacred sites, promoting sustainable practices, and sharing their knowledge of the natural world with others. By incorporating indigenous perspectives into environmental stewardship, conservationists can gain a deeper understanding of the cultural and ecological significance of Niagara Falls and work towards a more inclusive and holistic approach to conservation.

Finally, the protection of Niagara's natural beauty is also supported by legal protections and international cooperation. Because Niagara Falls straddles the border between the United States and Canada, both countries must work together to ensure its preservation. Binational agreements, such as the Boundary Waters Treaty of 1909 and the aforementioned Great Lakes Water Quality Agreement, provide frameworks for cooperation on issues such as water management, pollution control, and habitat restoration. These agreements reflect the shared responsibility of both nations to protect the falls and the surrounding environment, ensuring that future generations can continue to experience the awe and wonder of Niagara Falls in all its natural glory.

In conclusion, protecting Niagara's natural beauty is a multifaceted endeavor that requires the cooperation of governments, conservationists, indigenous communities, and the public. From managing water flow and pollution to controlling invasive species and promoting sustainable tourism, the efforts to preserve Niagara Falls reflect a deep commitment to maintaining this iconic natural wonder for generations to come. By balancing human activity with environmental stewardship, we can ensure that Niagara Falls remains a symbol of nature's power, beauty, and resilience, continuing to inspire awe and wonder for centuries to come.

Chapter 20: Fun Facts About Niagara Falls

Niagara Falls is one of the most iconic natural wonders of the world, captivating visitors with its awe-inspiring beauty and powerful rush of water. It draws millions of tourists each year from across the globe, and while many people are familiar with its stunning appearance, there are countless intriguing facts about Niagara Falls that reveal its history, formation, and unique characteristics. From the depths of its geological origins to the adventurous daredevils who have challenged its might, Niagara Falls holds a treasure trove of fascinating information. Let's explore a world of fun facts about Niagara Falls that highlight its grandeur and significance, both in nature and human history.

Niagara Falls, located on the border between the United States and Canada, is actually made up of three distinct waterfalls: Horseshoe Falls, American Falls, and Bridal Veil Falls. Horseshoe Falls, named for its horseshoe-shaped curve, is the largest of the three and spans the border between Ontario, Canada, and New York, USA. This waterfall is responsible for 90% of the water that flows over the falls, making it the most powerful waterfall in North America. American Falls, located entirely on the U.S. side, is the second largest, while Bridal Veil Falls is the smallest, located just next to American Falls, separated by Luna Island. Despite its smaller size, Bridal Veil Falls has its own charm, often capturing rainbows that delight visitors who catch them at the right angle.

One of the most amazing facts about Niagara Falls is the sheer volume of water that flows over the falls every second. It is estimated that about 3,160 tons of water flow over the falls every second, with the majority of this water plunging over Horseshoe Falls. To put this in perspective, the amount of water flowing over Niagara Falls in one minute could fill over 68 Olympic-sized swimming pools! This tremendous force makes Niagara Falls a symbol of raw, natural power. Over the years, various modifications have been made to control the flow of water for hydroelectric power generation, but the falls' impressive power is still visible to anyone who stands nearby and feels the thunderous vibrations of the water hitting the rocks below.

Despite its current location, Niagara Falls has not always been where it is today. Over thousands of years, the falls have been slowly retreating upstream due to the process of erosion. The falls were originally located about 7 miles (11 kilometers) downstream from their current location. The soft shale and limestone rock at the base of the falls are eroded by the force of the water, causing the falls to gradually move backward. It is estimated that Horseshoe Falls erodes at a rate of about 1 foot (30 centimeters) per year, although this rate has slowed in recent years due to engineering efforts that reduce the flow of water and help preserve the falls. The slow movement of the falls over millennia is a testament to the ever-changing nature of our planet's geological formations.

The height of Niagara Falls is another aspect that captures the imagination of visitors. Horseshoe Falls has a vertical drop of about 167 feet (51 meters), while American Falls drops 110 feet (34 meters), and Bridal Veil Falls has a similar drop of about 78 feet (24 meters). Although Niagara Falls is not the tallest waterfall in the world, it is the combination of height and volume that makes it so remarkable. The continuous rush of water and mist created by the falls produces a sensory experience unlike any other, with the sound of the water thundering in your ears and the cool spray misting your face as you stand in awe of this natural spectacle.

Another fun fact about Niagara Falls is that it serves as a major source of hydroelectric power for both the United States and Canada. The falls have been harnessed for power generation since the late 19th century, and today, the Niagara River's water is diverted to power plants that produce renewable electricity for millions of people.

Hydroelectric power from Niagara Falls played a crucial role in powering the factories and industries of the region during the 20th century, particularly during World War II when it was used to support wartime production. Even today, Niagara Falls remains an important source of clean energy, showcasing the incredible potential of nature to meet human needs sustainably.

Niagara Falls also has an interesting connection to the daredevils who have attempted to conquer it over the years. The first person to go over Niagara Falls in a barrel was a 63-year-old schoolteacher named Annie Edson Taylor in 1901. Taylor hoped that her stunt would bring her fame and fortune, but while she survived the fall, she did not achieve the lasting financial success she had hoped for. Over the years, other adventurers have followed in her footsteps, attempting to go over the falls in barrels, boats, and even jet skis. Some survived their daring attempts, while others were not so lucky. Despite the dangers, Niagara Falls continues to inspire thrill-seekers, although such stunts are now illegal without special permission.

The wildlife around Niagara Falls is another fascinating aspect that many visitors may not immediately notice. The region is home to a wide variety of species, including birds, mammals, reptiles, and fish. Niagara Falls serves as a crucial stopover point for migratory birds, and birdwatchers often flock to the area to observe species such as peregrine falcons, bald eagles, and ospreys. In the river below the falls, fish such as salmon and trout navigate the powerful waters, while beavers, otters, and raccoons can be found along the riverbanks. The rich biodiversity of the area is supported by the unique combination of freshwater habitats and forests that surround the falls, making it a vital ecosystem for wildlife.

Another fun fact about Niagara Falls is that it has frozen over several times in history, creating a stunning winter wonderland. One of the most famous incidents occurred in 1848, when an ice jam on Lake Erie stopped the flow of water over the falls for several hours.

While the falls did not completely freeze solid, the flow of water was reduced to a trickle, and people were able to walk out on the frozen riverbed to explore the area up close. More recently, in 2014 and 2015, the extreme cold temperatures caused parts of the falls to freeze again, creating spectacular ice formations that attracted thousands of visitors to see the "frozen falls." The icy scene looked like something out of a fantasy, with glistening ice and snow covering the landscape.

One of the lesser-known facts about Niagara Falls is that it has been a location for many famous movies and television shows. From romantic comedies to action films, Niagara Falls has provided a dramatic backdrop for countless cinematic moments. One of the most famous movies filmed at Niagara Falls was the 1953 thriller *Niagara*, starring Marilyn Monroe. The falls also appeared in the classic film *Superman II* (1980), where Superman saves a boy who falls over the edge of the falls. More recently, the falls were featured in movies like *Pirates of the Caribbean: At World's End* (2007) and *The Office* (American version) during Jim and Pam's iconic wedding episode. The timeless beauty and dramatic force of Niagara Falls make it a favorite filming location for directors seeking a natural wonder that adds both romance and intensity to their stories.

Niagara Falls has also played an important role in history, particularly in the relationship between the United States and Canada. During the War of 1812, the region around Niagara Falls was the site of several battles between American and British forces, including the famous Battle of Lundy's Lane. In the years that followed, Niagara Falls became a symbol of peace and cooperation between the two nations, with both the U.S. and Canada working together to protect and preserve the falls for future generations. The falls have been a destination for diplomats and leaders over the years, including a visit from British Prime Minister Winston Churchill during World War II and U.S. President Franklin D. Roosevelt, who celebrated the opening of a major hydroelectric power plant at Niagara Falls.

The cultural significance of Niagara Falls extends to indigenous communities, who have long viewed the falls as a sacred site. For the Haudenosaunee (Iroquois) people, particularly the Seneca Nation, Niagara Falls holds deep spiritual meaning, and their legends and stories about the falls have been passed down through generations. One famous legend tells of Lelawala, the Maid of the Mist, a young woman who sacrificed herself by going over the falls to appease the thunder god Hinum, who lived in the mist. The stories of Niagara Falls continue to be a vital part of indigenous culture, and today, many indigenous leaders are involved in efforts to protect the natural beauty of the falls and promote sustainable tourism practices that respect the land and its history.

In conclusion, Niagara Falls is not just a beautiful natural landmark; it is a place filled with rich history, fascinating geological formations, powerful energy, and a vibrant ecosystem. From the awe-inspiring force of the water to the thrilling tales of daredevils and the cultural significance of the falls, Niagara Falls offers endless fun facts that make it a truly unique destination. Whether you're visiting for the first time or have seen it many times before, there is always something new to learn and discover about this iconic natural wonder.

Epilogue

As our journey through Niagara Falls comes to an end, we hope you've discovered just how incredible this natural wonder truly is. From its powerful waters to its rich history, Niagara Falls is a place where nature, adventure, and awe come together in a way that few other places on Earth can match.

But Niagara Falls is more than just a waterfall—it's a symbol of the beauty and power of nature. It's a reminder of the importance of preserving our environment so that future generations can enjoy the same breathtaking views and thrilling experiences that people have been enjoying for hundreds of years.

Now that you know all about Niagara Falls, you can share your knowledge with friends and family, or even plan your own visit to see this amazing sight in person. Whether you're standing at the edge of the falls, feeling the mist on your face, or watching the colorful lights dance on the water at night, you'll appreciate the falls in a whole new way.

Thank you for joining us on this adventure. Remember, the wonders of Niagara Falls are always there, waiting to inspire and amaze you. So, until we meet again, keep exploring, keep learning, and keep marveling at the world around you!

The End.